£2–50
9a
5/21

Welfare Services

A guide for care workers

Pat Young

School of Health and Social Studies,
Colchester Institute

MACMILLAN

for Harry, Jake and Martin

First published 1993 by
THE MACMILLAN PRESS LTD
Houndmills, Basingstoke, Hampshire RG21 2XS
and London
Companies and representatives
throughout the world

ISBN 0–333–57539–3

A catalogue record for this book is available
from the British Library

Filmset by Wearset, Boldon, Tyne and Wear
Printed in Hong Kong

10 9 8 7 6 5 4 3 2 1
02 01 00 99 98 97 96 95 94 93

Contents

Acknowledgements

The author would like to thank those who have helped at various stages in the preparation of this book, in particular Ruth Felstead, Terry Smyth, Emma Lee, Michael Key, David Tossell, Richard Webb and Arthur Baker.

The author and publishers wish to thank the following for permission to use copyright material: BACUP – illustration, page 30; British Homoeopathic Association – illustration, page 57; Cancer Relief Macmillan Fund – photograph, page 41; Cancerlink – illustration, page 27; Carers' National Association – illustration, page 98; Centrepoint Soho – photograph, page 9; Controller of Her Majesty's Stationery Office for Crown Copyright material – pages 6, 7, 12, 16, 23, 28, 29, 60, 64, 69, 73, 74, 90, 101, 105, 109, 130; Disabled Living Centres Council – illustration, page 97; Disabled Living Foundation – illustrations, pages 89, 90, 96; General Council and Register of Osteopaths – illustration, page 56; General Dental Council – illustration, page 36; Margaret Hanton and Pre-school Playgroup Association – photograph, page 118; Peter Hayman and Lynda King (Rose Cottage Residential Home, Broughton, Cambs) – photograph, page 122; Health Education Authority – illustration, page 45; Louis Hellman – cartoon, page 88; Independent Living Fund – illustration, page 79: MIND – illustration, page 54; Pre-school Playgroup Association – illustration, page 117; Joseph Rowntree Foundation – Family Fund illustration, page 80; Shaftesbury House – illustrations, page 8; The Society of Chiropodists – illustrations, page 39; Suffolk County Council/Ipswich Social Services Department – illustration, page 94; Sam Tanner – photograph, page 98.

Every effort has been made to trace all copyright holders, but if any have been inadvertently overlooked the publishers will be pleased to make the necessary arrangement at the first opportunity.

1 About this book

The field of welfare is vast and complex. Many people are not aware of their rights and as a result do not get the best deal for themselves. The most vulnerable people often have the most difficulty in finding their way around the services, yet these are the very people who are likely to need the services most. Care workers can help by having enough knowledge to be able to assist their clients in finding out what their rights are and what services are available to them.

Recent trends in community care have increased the need for anyone working in care to have some knowledge of the welfare system. In the past, clients might have had all their needs met within one institution: now a complex package of care has to be put together by and for people living in the community. The package may include housing, income, health care, practical support, social activities and education or employment. The services involved are likely to include not just those within the welfare state, such as the National Health Service and social services, but also services provided by voluntary organisations and by the private sector. Community care also means that care workers have to function in a more independent way than before. A community psychiatric nurse, for example, will be part of a team of care workers, but she may well be the only person present when a client is distressed by a letter from her landlord giving her notice to quit.

Who is this book for?

The book will be helpful to you if you are already working in the care sector, if you are training for this kind of work, or if you are involved in caring in a more informal way – looking after a friend or relative, or as a volunteer worker.

- If you are employed as a full- or part-time worker in the health services, social services or with a voluntary organisation, you will find that it provides information which has a practical application in your work. You might use it while on an in-service training course.
- If you are preparing for assessment for a National Vocational Qualification (NVQ) or Scottish Vocational Qualification (SVQ), up to and including Level 3, the book will help. It gives you the knowledge necessary to show competence in areas such as enabling clients to make use of available services and information, an important part of the effective care of clients.
- If you are a full- or part-time student taking, for example, a BTEC, City & Guilds or CCETSW qualification, you will find that this book includes information you need on social policy and welfare legislation. All these courses include work experience: this book will help you to develop your skills and understanding in a practical context.

- If you are following a training course leading to a professional qualification, in occupational therapy or social work, for example, you will find that the book gives a useful summary of welfare provision.

The aims of the book

The book aims to give information on welfare rights and welfare services, and to link this information into the practice of care. It is not expected that you will become an expert in all the fields described in the book – a kind of do-it-yourself lawyer *cum* social security adviser *cum* doctor! Rather you will gain the knowledge and understanding to be able to direct a client to a source of help and to give you confidence in supporting a client in dealing with the services.

The structure of the book

There are six chapters, covering the key areas of housing, health, money, daily living, employment and children.

The first chapter looks at ways to find help with housing and describes the legal position of tenants and owner-occupiers. There is a section on homelessness. The chapter on health is mainly concerned with the National Health Service, although alternative medicine and private health care are also covered. The work of voluntary organisations is considered, as for example in the case of provision for people with AIDS.

The chapter on money deals mostly with welfare benefits; while that on daily living looks at services providing practical care for people with disabilities, and sources of support and information. The chapter on employment looks at ways of finding work or training for work, as well as ways of becoming involved in voluntary work. The final chapter, on children, examines various types of daycare and covers the legislation protecting children.

Each chapter includes a variety of activities and practical work to help you put the information into the context of care in practice.

How to use this book

This is not a book to be read from cover to cover. The way you use it will depend on your own particular situation and the kind of care you are involved in. The book can be used as a reference source, in your workplace or when you are on a training course. You may want to dip into various chapters, perhaps to learn about a new area or to refresh your memory on something with which you are already familiar. You might be directed to particular sections or exercises as part of an educational or training course. Some of the activities will need to be discussed with a tutor or supervisor and shared with colleagues. They can be adapted to suit your own situation and needs.

Some of the activities and exercises involve finding out about people and organisations. It is a good idea to check with your supervisor or tutor before tackling these, to make sure that you approach the right person, and that you have permission – if necessary – to do so.

Many of the activities involve finding out information and reflecting on it. To make the best use of this information and your experiences you will find it useful to get into the habit of keeping a written record of your learning. You will find the way which best suits your own purpose: a notebook or loose-leaf file, or perhaps a card-index system for some kinds of information. Your supervisor or tutor will guide you.

Terms used

Care worker is used to describe people employed in caring or who are training for employment in caring. **Carer** is used to refer to someone who cares for a friend or relative. The 'carer' needs to know about the system every bit as much as the 'care worker'. **Client** is used throughout when describing the person being cared for, although those working in the health services may be more used to using the term 'patient'.

Keeping up to date

Although there is considerable continuity in care work and in social policy, there is also a process of continual change. Laws are revised and updated; benefits are modified to suit changing circumstances; policies and practices are adapted. Recently there have been some rather more fundamental changes, affecting the philosophy behind the provision of welfare.

I have dealt with the changes in policy in two ways: by indicating, where possible, the direction of change which seems likely in the future; and by giving ways of updating information.

Voluntary organisations

The book includes an appendix listing the addresses of a large number of voluntary organisations, many of which work on shoestring budgets. Although these organisations will usually welcome enquiries, you should always send a stamped addressed envelope when you write for information, and be prepared to pay for leaflets and booklets.

2 Housing

Housing problems cut into all aspects of life. At the extreme there is the growing problem of homelessness. Without a home it is difficult to get and hold down a job. Homeless people cannot enjoy stable relationships or possessions. Even in temporary housing, such as bed and breakfast, the quality of family life is affected. Anxieties about the security and safety of housing also affect people's lives. Homelessness and worries about housing can be a cause of both physical and mental health problems.

People who are homeless or worried about losing their home need help and advice. There are many decisions to be made. There are agencies and people who can help; but a client may need advice about where to turn, and guidance and support through the maze of choices.

Problems to do with housing affect people in many varying situations. Each client is different and will be treated as such. The kind of advice and support offered will depend on the nature of your relationship to the client. Nurses in the fields of mental health and mental handicap (learning difficulties) help patients in transitions from hospital to the community. Housing is a key issue in a successful move to independent living. Young people leaving the care of the local authority need the support of residential and other social workers in making this move. Older people living on their own in the community may need to find a more sheltered form of housing and may seek the advice and support of their carers.

This chapter explains the various sources of advice and information on housing. You may use these yourself or refer a client to them. You may accompany a client on a visit; asking for help, especially when stressed, can be difficult. The chapter also explains, in outline, some aspects of the law on housing. You will not be competent to give legal advice – there are lawyers to do that – but at least you should know what rights people have. A client can then be advised to seek proper legal help.

2.1 Housing advice and information

There are several places which can give advice and information on housing problems. The ones described below should be available in most areas. There will also be services which are special to one local area.

Housing advice centres

Most towns have a **housing advice centre** (or 'housing aid centre'). These are run by the local council, but do not help only council tenants: they offer advice and information to all local people. The help is free. Housing advice centres can help with most kinds of housing problems, including homelessness, difficulties with rent, threatened repossession of a house, and domestic violence. The office is usually to be found in the town centre, perhaps in a converted shop.

Housing advice centres have information leaflets. They give personal advice on individual problems. They will also contact other parts of the council, or other organisations such as the Department of Social Security. In some cases they are able to represent clients in legal arguments with landlords or building societies.

Citizens' Advice Bureaux (CAB)

All parts of the UK have **Citizens' Advice Bureaux**. They can offer general advice and information on housing (as well as on many other matters). If more detailed advice is needed, the CAB will know where to go to find it. Many bureaux provide free appointments with a solicitor, usually one evening a week.

Solicitors

Names and addresses of solicitors can be found in the telephone book. Other organisations such as housing advice centres can also provide lists of solicitors, usually saying which offer **legal aid**. Solicitors provide legal advice. If someone is on Income Support or has a low income, he or she will be entitled to legal aid, which means that the services of the solicitor will be free. Even if the person is not entitled to legal aid, many solicitors offer a **fixed fee** appointment. This means that they will give up to half an hour's advice for a fixed cost (£5.00 in April 1992).

Local newspapers

Local newspapers have advertisements of places to rent and to buy. Libraries keep copies of these newspapers, which can be read by anyone, free.

Finding out more: housing

★ More general information on housing issues can be found from **Shelter**. Shelter is a voluntary organisation which campaigns for homeless people. It publishes many excellent leaflets and books. A list of these can be obtained by writing to Shelter.

★ There is also an advice service, **SHAC**, which specialises in advice on all aspects of housing.

TO DO

1 Make a survey of local sources of information on housing.

- Find out whether there is a housing advice centre. If there is, visit it if possible to see what services it offers and how 'user-friendly' the service is.
- Find the address and opening hours of the local CAB.
- Which local newspapers are the most useful, and on which days do most advertisements appear?
- Are there any local organisations offering advice and information, perhaps for a particular client group, such as young people?

Check what information is already available in your workplace. It may be that this task has already been done, but some updating may be needed. Keep a record of everything you find out.

2 What would be the best way to organise this information for other users? A box file? Or perhaps a computer database?

3 Can you make this information available to your clients as well as your colleagues?

2.2   Finding a home – types of housing

This section covers the various types of housing available. The choice will depend on the amount of money the client has, as well as other factors such as the availability of the different sorts of housing in the local area. The most obvious ways to get a home are to buy or to rent. Most people who buy do so with a mortgage from a bank or building society, but this is not the only way. Houses can be rented from private owners or from the council. In the rented sector there are also housing associations, which are a good source of reasonably priced housing. This section looks at these ways of finding housing, as well as housing co-operatives, shared-ownership schemes, and finding accommodation in hostels and nightshelters.

Buying a house

Some people buy their house outright. Most, though, have to borrow money for such an expensive purchase. **Mortgages** to buy a house can be sought from building societies, banks or the local authority. Finance companies will also lend money for housing, but they are not recommended as interest rates are higher. They are also less likely to be sympathetic if the person cannot meet the mortgage repayments.

Lenders vary as regards how much they are prepared to lend. The amount depends also on a number of other factors, to do with the circumstances of the borrower and the type of property to be bought. As a rough guide, someone could expect to borrow two-and-a-half to three times their gross income. People on Income Support are able to get a mortgage on the basis of their benefit payments: in these cases the Department of Social Security will usually pay the interest on the loan.

In some cases, for instance after a house has been repossessed by a building society or bank or where the income seems very insecure, it may be necessary to have a **guarantor** for a mortgage. The guarantor is someone who agrees to be responsible for the mortgage if the payments are not made. Local authorities can take this role – either through the 1985 Housing Act, or through social services. Social services can help if there is a child in the family and buying a house will prevent the family from becoming homeless.

The 'right to buy'

The 'right to buy'

The 1980 Housing Act brought in the right for council tenants to buy their homes. This right applies after two years and most homes are eligible, but not sheltered housing. Tenants get a discount on the price – 32 per cent after two years, rising to 60 per cent after thirty years (April 1992 rates). The discount on flats is higher, starting at 44 per cent and rising to 70 per cent. If the house is sold within three years, part of the discount must be repaid.

Tenants wishing to buy are also entitled to a mortgage. This can be up to 100 per cent of the loan. The income on which the calculation is based can include several members of a family, such as two parents and a grown-up and working son or daughter who also lives there. If the council does not provide the loan itself, it will arrange for a building society to provide it.

Shared ownership

Many people will find that their income is too low to allow them to borrow enough money to buy even the smallest house. **Shared ownership** schemes are a way of helping less well-off people to buy a home. Most are operated by local authorities or by housing associations. The ownership of the property is shared between the individual occupier and the organisation. The occupier pays off a mortgage in the usual way on his or her own share of the property, and also pays rent on the remainder. The occupier's share of the ownership can be increased as time goes on.

Shared ownership schemes make buying a home cheaper

Housing co-operatives

A **housing co-operative** is a group of people who manage and control the housing they live in. Everyone is equal in the co-op and no one individually owns the property or makes money out of anyone else. Everyone pays a fair share of the costs. Usually the property is collectively owned by the co-op, although there are also management co-ops. In such cases, the property is owned by a council or housing association, but all the day-to-day running of the housing is managed by the co-op. Grants are available towards the cost of establishing a co-op: these are provided by the government, through the housing corporation.

Housing co-ops have many benefits. They are a means of achieving decent housing. They are a way of avoiding the 'red tape' of council housing. They give people power over their own homes, with shared responsibility. A housing co-op often gives a much greater sense of community to the residents than any other kind of housing. However, co-ops also involve the hard work of co-operating with others over the management of the housing. This involves a certain amount of commitment.

Privately rented housing

This is perhaps the simplest way of finding somewhere to live. It suits people who do not want the ties of owning a house. It is however an expensive option, and gives the occupant few rights over his or her housing. A lot of the people who rent privately do so because they cannot find anything better. Rented property can be found through an agency, or through local newspapers. Shop noticeboards also often have advertisements of rooms to rent. Housing Benefit can be claimed by tenants on a low income or Income Support (see Chapter 3). A later section in this chapter describes the rights and duties both of landlords or landladies and of tenants.

Council housing

It is increasingly difficult to get a council house or flat. Councils have lost a lot of property as a result of having to sell houses to tenants. They are also under a legal obligation to house people classed as homeless (see section 2.5). In deciding who to house, councils operate a **points system**. People who apply to the council are allocated a certain number of points, depending on their circumstances, their needs and their present housing. The number of points determines where the person is placed on the waiting list. This in turn decides how quickly, if ever, the person will be offered a house or a flat. A single childless person in good health, for example, has very little chance of being housed.

Tenants of the council have rights, under the 1980 Housing Act. They have **security of tenure** (they cannot be evicted without there being certain reasons and procedures); they have the right to sub-let and to improve the property; and they have the right to receive certain information. After two years, tenants have the right to buy their home (see earlier). Tenants can swap council houses, and there is a national computerised scheme to help people to contact each other.

The 1988 Housing Act brought in a scheme whereby tenants can vote to have a different landlord. There is also provision under this Act for trusts to be set up by the government to take over the most run-down estates. These trusts are called **Housing Action Trusts** (**HATs**). The intention was that they would improve the estate over a period of five years and then pass it on to a new landlord. Neither of these schemes has so far proved to be very popular with tenants. As a result, new schemes are being developed involving housing associations.

Housing associations

There are about half a million flats and houses owned and rented out by housing associations in Britain. A **housing association** is a non-profit-making organisation which aims to provide good-quality housing at a reasonable rent for people who might not otherwise find such housing. Some

Living in a housing association home

Reception at a shelter for young people in London

housing associations are small and locally based; others are larger. They offer various sorts of housing, including flats and houses and also sheltered housing and hostel-type schemes. Some properties are newly built; some are converted and renovated. Many housing associations help people with special needs, such as people with disabilities.

There are various ways in which people get into housing-association property. Some people are nominated by the council: this is the case for about 50 per cent of housing-association tenants. Sometimes housing advice centres can nominate tenants. Some housing associations have waiting lists. The housing association will interview people applying and will usually make its decision on the basis of need.

Tenants of housing associations are given more rights than is required by the law. They do not, however, have the right to buy. But a tenant who wants to buy a house can apply for financial help. This is a kind of transferable discount scheme.

Hostels and nightshelters

Most towns have various **hostels**. These range from Women's Aid houses, for women who have suffered violence from their partners, to hostels run by the social services departments for people with psychiatric problems. Some hostels are run by voluntary organisations, some by the local authority, and some by private organisations. They are usually for people with special needs of some kind. Some are for young people who find themselves homeless. Hostels usually offer rooms to rent and many provide support and guidance as well as a roof.

Nightshelters provide temporary accommodation for homeless people. They are usually run by voluntary organisations. Often the shelter is limited by age and sex. Some shelters are specifically for young people; others will not accept people under a certain age. The shelters usually offer washing and laundry facilities. The staff are accepting and sympathetic, although basic rules such as a ban on alcohol and drugs are strictly followed.

WORDCHECK

housing advice centre A centre that offers free advice on all aspects of housing.

legal aid A scheme under which people with a low income can receive free advice from a solicitor.

voluntary organisation An organisation which has not been set up by the government and which does not aim to make a profit.

mortgage A loan to buy a house: the house is used as security on the loan and can therefore be repossessed if the loan is not paid.

housing association A voluntary organisation which provides housing for rent.

housing co-operative A group of people managing their own housing collectively.

shared ownership A scheme which allows people to buy part of a house or flat and to rent the other part.

guarantor A person who takes responsibility for someone else's loan.

nightshelter A centre that provides very basic overnight accommodation for homeless people.

Housing Benefit A benefit to help with the costs of rent, for people on a low income.

points system A system used by local councils in allocating housing.

Housing Action Trusts (HATs) Trusts set up by the government to take over run-down council estates.

security of tenure The right of a tenant to remain in his or her home.

Finding out more: buying a house

★ The Department of the Environment publishes an attractive and readable booklet which is a guide to buying a council house or flat. It is called *Your Right to Buy Your House*, and is available from the local council or CAB.

★ There are several types of housing co-operatives. These are described, along with other details, in a leaflet called *Housing Co-operatives*, produced by the Housing Corporation.

★ The Housing Corporation also offers a leaflet called *Shared Ownership*.

Finding out more: self-build schemes

★ Another way into home-ownership is with self-build schemes. The Housing Corporation publishes a leaflet which explains how these work and what help is available. Information is also available from The Community Self-Build Agency, and from the National Federation for Housing Associations.

TO DO

Select three of your clients. Consider their housing needs. Make a list of all the forms of housing available to each client.

- What would be the advantages and disadvantages of each type of housing?
- How would you advise the client to find out details of each type of housing?

(If you work with older people, you may wish to read the final section of this chapter before doing this exercise.)

2.3 Tenants' rights

This section looks at the law which relates to renting a home. More than half of the population of Britain owns a house; many others rent their home from a private owner, and it is likely that care workers will be involved more often with those who are renting.

Some people choose to rent: perhaps they do not want the responsibility of owning a house; perhaps they are renting temporarily – because of a short-term job, or before deciding to buy. Many people, however, rent from a private owner because they have no choice. There are many reasons for this. One is that council houses are becoming harder to find, as more and more are sold off to existing tenants. Another is that not everyone qualifies for a mortgage to buy a house: a certain level of secure income is needed. Young people leaving the care of the local authority are unlikely to be able to buy a house, unless they have a very well paid job. They would not qualify for council housing without children, unless in poor health or perhaps under a special scheme for young people. Older people who have been used to renting may continue to rent, as this was more popular in the past. People leaving institutions such as psychiatric hospitals or mental-handicap hospitals are unlikely to be in a position to buy. There may be special schemes provided by the health authority, by the social services or by a voluntary organisation, but often these are inadequate to meet the need.

It is useful for care workers to know something of the rights which tenants have under the law. Many tenants do not know their rights, or how to make use of their rights. Support and advice may be needed, especially by vulnerable people such as those with learning difficulties. By knowing something of the law, it is possible that you could help to prevent someone from becoming homeless. And this in itself could avert a number of other problems.

The rights considered here fall into three main areas. Firstly there is the law concerning **security of tenure** – in other words, the tenant's right to stay in his or her home and the rights of the owner to evict a tenant. This is perhaps the most important area, but also the most complicated. The second area concerns rent. There are some laws about the amounts of rent which can be charged by an owner. The final area concerns repairs to the property – the obligations both of the owner and of the tenant.

Housing law is complicated. This is mainly because successive governments have passed a number of different Acts over the years. Some of these have given tenants more rights: some have substantially reduced their rights. When a new law comes in, it affects new tenancies from a particular date. People already renting their home continue to be under the old law and have the old rights. More recent laws have taken away some tenants' rights, so people who begin to rent a house now will probably have fewer rights than those who have been renting for a long time. An important date in this is 15 January 1989, since this is when the 1988 Housing Act came into effect.

Evictions

Tenancies created before 15 January 1989

Most tenancies where the tenant moved in before 15 January 1989 are Rent Act-protected tenancies. It is harder for an owner to get a tenant out of these tenancies than from a more recent letting.

Two things must happen before a tenant can be evicted:

- A tenant must be given a **notice to quit**. This is a formal document which must allow at least four weeks' notice and which must tell the tenant that legal advice is available. It might be a good idea for a solicitor to check whether the document has been compiled properly; if not, it is not legally binding.
- The owner must get a **possession order** from the court. This is only given if certain grounds, or reasons, can be proven.

There are six situations in which the court will always give the property back to the owner, regardless of the effect on the tenant. One example of these is when an owner-occupier wants to move back into the house. Another is where the property is classed as either a holiday let or a shorthold tenancy.

There are also discretionary grounds for eviction. In these cases the court will take account of the *reasonableness* of the decision. It would look, for example, at the behaviour of the owner and of the tenant, and also at the needs of each. If the tenant had children, the effects of eviction on the children would be taken into account. Examples of these grounds are:

- not paying the rent;
- sub-letting;
- keeping pets when this is not allowed;
- annoying the neighbours, for example with late-night parties.

There are also reasons to do with the **convenience** to the owner. In other words the court will consider whether the owner has a good reason for wanting the property back. Examples of these are:

- the tenant was employed by the owner and now the owner needs the property for a new worker;
- the tenant earlier gave notice that he or she was going to leave and the owner made arrangements for a new tenant to move in.

Tenancies created after 15 January 1989

In 1988 a new Housing Act was passed. The government wanted to make more houses available to rent. It believed that people were put off from renting houses out because they were worried that tenants could not be evicted. So the new law makes it easier for owners to get tenants out. Another important change concerned rents; this is considered on page 13.

The new tenancies are called **assured tenancies**. To repossess the house the owner must still get a court order, but no notice to quit is required. The

A solicitor can help with a housing problem

Tenants can be evicted if they break the rules of the tenancy

owner serves a notice that he or she intends to repossess the house, and tells the tenant the reason. If the reason concerns something the tenant has done wrong, court proceedings can start after two weeks. In other cases the owner must wait for two months.

The grounds for repossession of assured tenancies are similar to those for protected tenancies, but they are more generous to the owner. In some cases the owner must let the tenant know from the beginning that the property may be repossessed. The grounds where this is the case include the following:

- the owner lived in the house before it was rented out: no reason for wanting the house back needs to be given;
- the owner has a mortgage on the house which he or she cannot pay, and the house cannot be sold with tenants living in it.

With the following reasons, the tenant does not have to be warned at the beginning of the tenancy:

- the owner needs to do major repairs which cannot be done with the tenant living there, or the owner wants to knock the house down;
- at least three weeks' rent has not been paid.

The *discretionary* grounds – where the court will examine the situation of the owner and the tenant – include cases in which the tenant:

- owes rent;
- has often delayed in paying the rent;
- has not looked after the property.

The law also allows for short-term lets. These are called **assured shorthold tenancies**. With a shorthold tenancy it is agreed at the beginning that the tenancy will be for a fixed period of time (at least six months). Unless the tenant or the owner breaks the agreed rules of the contract in some way, neither can end the tenancy before the time is up.

In all of the situations described above it would be a good idea for a tenant who is threatened with an eviction to consult a solicitor. This should be done as soon as possible.

A final point worth mentioning here is that social services departments can make payments to prevent children from coming into care. This is called **Section 1 money**, because it is referred to in Section 1 of the 1980 Child Care Act. Although social services do not have very much Section 1 money, it can be used to prevent homelessness by paying off rent arrears, if this would mean a child did not have to come into care.

Rents

Again the situation regarding rents varies according to the type of tenancy.

Tenancies created before 15 January 1989

These are **protected tenancies**, under the 1977 Rent Act. With this type of tenancy, a fair rent can be set. The fair rent is decided by the rent officer, an employee of the local council. Either the owner or the tenant can apply for a **fair rent** to be set; this rent will then be registered. The decision about the amount of rent is made on the basis of the property – the size, condition, and so on. The decision is not influenced by the scarcity of places to rent. In other words a high rent will not be set just because there is nowhere else to live and people are so desperate they will pay any amount to have a home.

TO DO

1 Arrange to visit the local court on a day when repossession hearings are being heard. These are heard in the county court and the telephone number is listed in the *Yellow Pages*, under 'Courts'.

2 Listen to a number of cases. Notice what the court is taking note of.

Courts can be intimidating places – even when you're not being accused of anything – so you might want to do this exercise with a colleague.

TO THINK ABOUT

What rights would the people in the following situations have?

(a) Mr and Mrs Westover, both aged 63, have lived in a rented house for the last twenty years. The owner wants them out so that he can sell the property without tenants.

(b) Samantha and her child live in a flat they have rented since 1980. The owner wants them to move out so that his son can live there. The son has recently married.

(c) A young man, Winston, has been using his flat for weekly all-night parties. He is also behind with his rent. The owner has told him he must leave.

(d) For the past year, Sharma, a student, has rented a house on a shorthold lease. The lease is now up, and Sharma finds that she is pregnant, and with nowhere else to go.

Tenancies created after 15 January 1989

These are **assured tenancies**, under the 1988 Housing Act. At the beginning of the tenancy, the owner is entirely free to set any rent he or she likes. The only control applies to rent increases *after* the tenant has moved into the property. After a year the owner can raise the rent. If the tenant is not happy about this, he or she can go to the **Rent Assessment Committee**. They will assess the rent, on the basis of the current rent if the house or flat was to be re-let – in other words, the Rent Assessment Committee will try to set the current market value.

With an **assured shorthold tenancy** the tenant does not have to wait for the owner to increase the rent. He or she can go immediately to the Rent Assessment Committee who will decide what the market rent should be.

Repairs

The owner has a responsibility to keep the basic structure of the house or flat in good repair. The owner's duties include the upkeep of:

- drains, gutters and pipes;
- the supply of gas, electricity and water;
- heating systems and water heating;
- toilets, sinks, baths and showers.

The owner does not have to make repairs if the damage has been done by the tenant, however. Decorating inside is the responsibility of the tenant. And it is up to the tenant to report any repairs that need doing, and then to allow the owner access to inspect and to make repairs.

If the owner does not keep the property in good condition, he or she can be sued in court. Another way is to involve the council. The environmental health department of the council will prosecute an owner whose property is a danger to health. The council can require an owner to make a property fit for habitation. If the owner ignores this, the council can do the work itself and get the money back from the owner.

WORDCHECK

security of tenure The right of a tenant to remain in his or her home.
notice to quit A formal document which tells a tenant that the owner intends to take back the property.
possession order A document from the court granting the right to repossess a home.
protected tenancy An older type of tenancy which gives the tenants more rights than other types.
assured tenancy A relatively new kind of rented property from which the tenant can more easily be evicted.
shorthold tenancy A tenancy agreement for a short term only.
Section 1 money Money which can be paid out by social services to prevent a child coming into care.
fair rent Rent set on a protected tenancy by the local rent officer.

Finding out more: tenants and the law

★ For a more detailed explanation of the law relating to rented property, see Hugh Brayne and Gerry Martin's *Law for Social Workers* (Blackstone Press: second edition, 1991).

TO THINK ABOUT

What rights would the people in the following situations have?

(a) A family who are renting a house are troubled by a seriously leaking roof.

(b) A man has recently moved into a flat, with an agreed rent of £200 a month. As soon as he had settled in, the owner raised the rent to £300.

TO DO

Consider any clients you have who live in rented property, and try to find out something about their situations.

- What kind of tenancies do they have?
- What rights do they have? In what circumstances could they be evicted?

2.4 Problems with mortgages

More and more people are buying houses with loans from banks or building societies. This is partly because it has become harder to find homes to rent – as more council houses are sold off and fewer places are available to rent privately. But it is also because government policies have encouraged people to buy. Council-house rents have increased. Tenants of private owners have fewer and fewer rights. Many people have bought council houses, with very generous discounts and 100 per cent mortgages.

Many people have benefited from buying their own home. But as the number of owners has increased, so too has the number of people experiencing problems in repaying mortgages. In earlier days owner-occupation was an option taken up by better-off people with secure jobs. It was very rare for people to default on their mortgages and for the building society to repossess the house. Now the extension of owner-occupation to less well-off people has changed things. It is becoming increasingly common for banks and building societies to repossess houses.

Unemployment is often the reason people can no longer pay their mortgage. As unemployment rises, so do repossessions. Unemployment has hit hard in recent years – even in areas of work where people thought they were safe. Another common cause of mortgage **arrears** is separation and divorce. Often the woman is left in the house but is unable to go on paying the mortgage.

Losing a home

This section explains what happens if someone cannot meet his or her mortgage repayments. It also describes the best strategy for people wishing to keep their home. Although some people decide to give up their home – finding the worry of trying to meet mortgage repayments too much to cope with – there are disadvantages to this course of action. The most obvious is that the person loses the home and may not find it easy to find another. The council may consider people to be 'intentionally homeless' if they have voluntarily given back a home they owned. In this case the council do not have to provide permanent accommodation. A drop in house prices may mean that the house is sold for less than the buying price, leaving the owner in debt to the building society or bank. When building societies sell houses, they do not always get the best deal possible and money may be lost in this way. Finally, someone who has had a house repossessed may find it difficult to get any kind of credit afterwards and hard to get another mortgage at a later date.

Stages of repossession

If the repayments on a mortgage are not made, the lender – the bank, the building society or whatever – is entitled to apply to the court to evict the owner. The house will then be sold to pay off the loan. Any money left over will go to the owner. For this to happen, a number of procedures have to be followed. Note, however, that *the process can be stopped at any time.*

Stage 1
When repayments stop, the building society will write, asking that the payments be brought up to date.

Stage 2
The building society will write again, threatening legal action.

Stage 3
The building society will pass details to its solicitors. The solicitors will contact the court.

Stage 4
The court will issue a **summons**. This will give a date for the hearing.

Stage 5
The court hearing. A number of options are possible:

- Arrears are paid: no possession order is issued.
- Arrears to be paid in the future: a *suspended* possession order is issued.
- A possession order is issued. This sets a date, usually within 28 days, for repossession.

Stage 6
On the day set, the lender applies for a **possession warrant**. The court gives details to its officials – the **bailiffs** – who decide a date and time. They inform the owner-occupier.

Stage 7
If the house is still occupied when the bailiffs arrive, they will evict the owner.

Avoiding repossession

There are various things which owner-occupiers can do if they are having difficulty in paying the mortgage. The ideal time to take action is at the very beginning. It is best not to stop paying the mortgage, even if the full amount

Get in touch with the building society

cannot be paid. The owner should get in touch with the building society or bank. It may be able to help by *rearranging* the mortgage. Building societies do not want to evict people and repossess homes. It is trouble for them. And they can be quite flexible in making decisions.

The details of how mortgages can be rearranged depends on the type of mortgage involved. A **capital repayment mortgage** works in a different way from an **endowment mortgage**. With a capital repayment mortgage, two courses of action are possible:

- to pay the interest only, for a period of time;
- to make a new mortgage arrangement over a longer period of time – this would mean lower monthly payments.

An endowment mortgage is less flexible. For this reason it may be best to swap to a capital repayment mortgage. As an alternative, it may be possible to stop paying the policy premiums for a short period of time. It is unlikely that this could continue for more than six months.

Once the lender has started the procedure of repossessing the house, it is still possible to stop the process. Although this can be done at any stage, it is important not to delay. If the bank or building society is sending threatening letters, but has not yet applied for a court hearing, the owner should contact the bank or building society. An offer should be made to clear the arrears and a promise made concerning future payments. As described above, the building society can be asked to help in reducing the payments.

After the court summons has arrived, it is possible to ask for an **adjournment**. This will allow time to work out a plan. The best way is to write to the building society's solicitors to ask them to agree to delay whilst negotiations take place. If they refuse, it is still possible for the court to agree to an adjournment. It is possible to ask the court to allow an adjournment at the actual hearing. Since it may not agree, though, the owner should be prepared to present his or her case anyway.

Even when a possession order or warrant has been made, it is possible for the court to prevent an eviction. New proposals can be offered at a further hearing.

Paying arrears

In order to keep the house, the owner must show how the arrears can be paid off.

- This can be done with a lump sum, or arrangements can be made for gradual repayments over a set period of time. If the person is on Income Support, the interest payments and an amount towards the arrears can be deducted from the benefit and paid directly to the lender.
- Social services have the power to give money if by doing so a child could be prevented from coming into care. This is under Section 1 of the 1980 Child Care Act. Although social services do not have a very big budget, this money can be used to prevent a family becoming homeless, if homelessness might mean a child coming into care.
- There are a number of charities which can give grants for particular purposes. Most libraries have a copy of *The Directory of Grant-Making Trusts*, which lists and briefly describes these charities.
- The building society may be persuaded to add the arrears to the capital already owed. This money can then be repaid through increased monthly repayments.

Two recent developments are important here:

- In the future, the Income Support which can be claimed for interest payments on a mortgage will be paid directly to the building society or bank.
- A scheme has been set up whereby housing associations may buy homes which might otherwise be repossessed. These are then rented to the owner-occupier, to be bought back in the future.

WORDCHECK

possession order A document from the court granting the right to repossess a home.
arrears Money owed.
capital repayment mortgage A type of mortgage whereby the borrower pays back monthly sums which consist of interest and the loan itself.
endowment mortgage A type of mortgage in which the capital of the loan is paid off at the end of the period through an insurance policy.
summons A letter from the court informing the recipient of the date of a hearing.
bailiffs Representatives of the court, who have power to enforce a possession order.
adjournment An agreement by the court to delay proceedings until a later date.

Finding out more: problems with mortgages

★ SHAC publishes an excellent book of advice for home-owners. As well as explaining in more detail what to do if there are problems with mortgage repayments, it covers ways of increasing income by claiming benefits and other measures. It is regularly updated, and published in association with the Child Poverty Action Group. The title is *Rights Guide for Home-Owners*. It is available from SHAC or Shelter.

TO DO

Find a copy of *The Directory of Grant-Making Trusts*, which is probably available in your local library. Look at the range of organisations involved, and the purposes for which they offer grants. Are there any charities which could be useful to any of your clients?

2.5 Homelessness

People can become homeless for many reasons. Newspapers and television cameras have shown the increasing numbers of young people who sleep rough on the streets of London and other towns in Britain. Some of these people have run away from sexual and other forms of abuse at home. Some have been thrown out by their parents or step-parents. Until they are eighteen it is difficult for them to claim any money from social security (see Chapter 4 for details). A high proportion of young homeless people have been in the care of social services and have no parental home. Others cannot go home because their parents have divorced and remarried, and will no longer house them.

About one in eight people who become homeless have had to leave a room, flat or house they have been renting. People who rent their home have no right to stay on after the agreement ends, even if they have nowhere else to go (see section 2.3).

The fastest-growing kind of homelessness is where people can no longer pay a mortgage and the house is taken back by the lender. The rise in interest rates has made it harder for people to pay their mortgages. Unemployment too can mean the loss of a home. (See section 2.4 for advice on what to do when a mortgage cannot be paid.)

Homelessness and the law

The law says that the local authority – that is, the borough or district council – has certain duties towards homeless people. To qualify for help from the council the person must have no accommodation in which they are entitled to live, or be threatened with homelessness in the next 28 days. A woman would be seen as homeless if she cannot live with her husband because he is violent.

What the local authority must do for a homeless person depends on the situation and the reasons why he or she is homeless. The first decision which the council must make is whether or not the person is in **priority need**. There are four situations in which a person is classified as being in priority need:

- when a woman is expecting a baby;
- when there are children in the family;
- when the homeless person is older, mentally ill, handicapped, or seen as vulnerable for some other reason;
- when homelessness is caused by a fire, flood or other emergency.

The second decision the council makes is whether or not the person's homelessness is intentional: did the person do something which made him or her homeless? **Intentional homelessness** would include somebody who did not manage his or her money very well, who got into arrears with the rent, and who was evicted as a result. The homeless person can apply to the High Court for a review if he or she does not agree with what the council says.

The results of these decisions determine the council's duties to the homeless person. If a homeless person is in priority need he or she must be housed by the council. This could be in local authority housing or through another organisation such as a housing association. The accommodation should be permanent. The 1983 Code of Guidance issued by the government says that temporary housing, such as bed and breakfast, should be for a minimum period. This is not always what happens in practice. Many

CASE STUDIES

Imagine that the following people are clients of yours. What would you advise? What options are available, and what are the advantages and disadvantages of each?

(a) Debbie is sixteen. She is desperately unhappy at home since her mother remarried. She tells you she wants to move out.

(b) Mandy and Leon have been married for one year. They each had a well-paid job and so they were able to buy an expensive flat. Now Mandy is pregnant and wants to give up her job, and yesterday Leon's firm made him redundant.

(c) Ted has mild learning difficulties. He has been for several years a lodger in a house belonging to Mrs Nash, a widow aged 70. Her relatives have now suggested that she move in with them and sell her own house. Mrs Nash has agreed to do this, but is concerned about Ted.

councils are in a desperate situation: they are forced by law to help homeless people, but they have also been forced to sell council houses and restricted in their spending on new buildings. The local authorities have no housing to offer homeless people. For this reason many people are in fact housed in bed and breakfast or other unsuitable accommodation, often for a year or more. And this is at a great cost to the council.

When someone is threatened with homelessness, the local authority should try to prevent this person becoming homeless. This could be done by involving social services to help with family problems. If it seemed that a child might become homeless and have to go into care, social services could pay rent arrears to prevent eviction. If nothing works, then the local authority must provide housing.

If the council considers the person to be intentionally homeless, the council does not have to provide permanent accommodation. It is only required to provide temporary housing and advice and assistance. This only applies to people in priority need. People who are not in priority need – whether intentionally homeless or not – are only entitled to advice and assistance.

The final point concerns the part of the law which refers to a 'local connection'. This does not mean that people have to have a connection with the area in which they are applying for help: what it does mean is that if they have a connection with another local authority's area, the council can pass the problem on to that area.

WORDCHECK

local authority The local council, which in the case of housing could be a borough or district council.
intentional homelessness Homelessness deliberately caused by the client: the legislation on homelessness gives the local authority different and lesser duties in such cases.
priority need A condition in which the client, when homeless, *must* be provided by the council with housing.

Finding out more: homelessness

★ For a more detailed account of the law in relation to homelessness, see *Law for Social Workers*, by Hugh Brayne and Gerry Martin (Blackstone: second edition, 1991).

TO THINK ABOUT

What would be the duties of the council towards the people in the following situations?

(a) A girl of seventeen who is pregnant, and whose mother and step-father refuse to let her live with them.

(b) A couple whose agreement to rent their house is ending: the owner is going to sell the house.

(c) A couple with a baby, who are being evicted by the owner of their house. They got into debt after buying a car and couldn't pay the rent.

(d) A newly married couple with nowhere to go.

TO FIND OUT

1 What happens to homeless people in your area? The local authority housing department should be able to help you to answer these questions:

• How many homeless people are known to the housing department?
• What accommodation does the council use to house homeless people?
• How many people are in bed-and-breakfast accommodation?
• How long do people usually have to stay in temporary accommodation?

2 It might be possible to visit the council's temporary housing and bed-and-breakfast accommodation. If you can, look at what is provided.

• How much space do people have?
• Do any facilities have to be shared?
• Can food be prepared?
• Are there rules that restrict what residents can do?
• What difficulties do people face if living there?

2.6 Older people – special housing needs

Many of the people helped by the caring professions are older people. They mostly live in their own homes in the community. They may have the support and help of social workers, home helps, district nurses and other community carers.

Older people often have special housing needs. The houses they live in are more likely to be old and in poor condition. Older people sometimes live in houses originally bought for a young family, which are not suited to the needs of an older person living alone. Sometimes an older person may become too frail to live alone. Some older people feel very insecure on their own, and feel the need to know that help is closer to hand. This section considers the possibilities open to older people who need more care than is provided in ordinary housing.

Sheltered housing

Sheltered housing has become increasingly popular. It meets the needs of people who want to continue to have the independence of living in their own home, but who want some extra security along with fewer of the responsibilities of independent living.

A sheltered-housing scheme has a warden living on the premises. The warden keeps an eye on the residents, reports any maintenance or repair problems, and organises the use of any communal facilities. Most schemes have an alarm system or intercom from each flat or bungalow to the warden's office, and the warden will summon outside help if necessary.

Sheltered housing is specifically designed to meet the needs of older people and will usually have such features as waist-height plug sockets, lifts as well as stairs, and handles on baths. The maintenance of the building and of the gardens is provided, and paid for with a service charge. There will usually be communal facilities such as a laundry and a lounge. Schemes also provide a guest room for visitors.

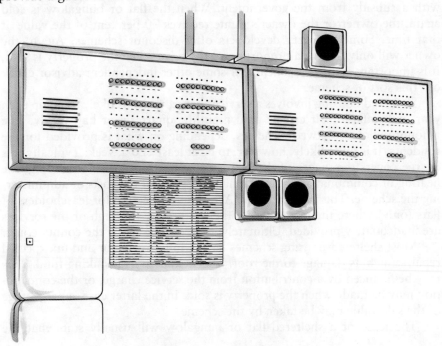

Alarm system connected to warden's office

A small amount of sheltered housing is available to rent from local authorities and from housing associations. This is not enough to meet the demand. Private developers have responded to the growing need by building private sheltered-housing schemes, this housing being for sale. This section therefore concentrates on sheltered housing which is owner-occupied rather than that which is rented.

Owner-occupation

Some people, having sold a house which they have owned, are able to buy outright. For people who cannot buy outright, there are a number of options. Housing associations run **leasehold** schemes, where the older person buys a 70 per cent share of the lease. The other 30 per cent is funded with a subsidy from the government. When the flat or bungalow is sold again, the owner or the owner's estate receives 70 per cent of the value at that time. Some property developers offer discount schemes. Again, the owner will only receive a proportion of the price when the property is sold. It is important to have a solicitor or some other independent advisor check out this sort of scheme.

Sheltered housing involves a **service charge**, which is likely to go up each year with inflation. It can be paid monthly, quarterly or half-yearly. The amount will vary between schemes, depending on what is provided for the residents. It is quite likely, however, to be at least £20 a week. Typically this charge covers the wages of the warden, the insurance of the building, the heating of communal areas, maintenance costs, and the costs of administering the scheme. The 1980 Housing Act offers protection for leaseholders of flats (only) where the residents feel the charges are too high or the services are inadequately provided. Ultimately, these can be set by the county court.

Most sheltered-housing schemes have a fund for major and unexpected repairs, such as damage to the roof. This is known as a **sinking fund**. This may be financed by a contribution from the service charge, or the contribution may be made when the property is sold. In the latter case, a percentage of the sale value may be taken by the scheme.

The lease of a sheltered flat or bungalow will usually state that the property must be sold to someone over a certain age. The management committee may have to approve a buyer and may itself do the selling.

Sheltered-housing schemes do not offer help with personal care or domestic tasks. But older people in sheltered housing can still make use of other services such as home helps, meals-on-wheels and community nursing services. Some schemes make a provision to move a resident out if he or she becomes very confused or in some way disruptive.

Sheltered housing with extra care

This is sometimes called **very sheltered housing** and is sometimes known as **extra-care sheltered housing**. Such schemes work on the same principles as sheltered housing, allowing people the freedom and independence of living in their own home, but also provide extra services such as meals and greater support. There is not yet very much of this type of provision. That which does exist tends to be provided by local authorities or housing associations.

These schemes do not provide nursing care. An older person needing this level of care may have to consider a move into a residential or nursing home.

Finding out more: sheltered housing

★ Age Concern publishes an excellent booklet called *Housing Options for Older People*. This explains the different kinds of housing available, advises on ways money can be raised from a home, and discusses ways of getting repairs done.

★ Age Concern and the National Housing and Town Planning Council have produced a very useful booklet called *A Buyer's Guide to Sheltered Housing*. It gives information on all aspects of sheltered housing and includes details of other useful publications and addresses of organisations that can supply more information.

A useful booklet for older people

Residential homes

There are three types of homes for older people: those run by the local authorities; those run by private organisations for profit; and those run by voluntary organisations. In all cases the homes vary a great deal, in terms both of the type of accommodation and of the standard of care offered.

Local authority homes

It is quite difficult to get into a local authority elderly people's home. Pressure on places means that only those with the greatest need will be accepted.

Local authority homes are run by the social services departments. Local authority homes are sometimes known as **Part III accommodation**. This is because it was in Part III of the 1948 National Assistance Act that the government said that local authorities must provide accommodation for 'persons who by reason of age, infirmity, or any other circumstances are in need of care and attention which is not otherwise available to them'.

A home run by a local authority generally caters for at least twenty people; some are much larger. Some are purpose-built, others are converted from older buildings. There is usually an officer-in-charge, who is a trained social worker, and various other care staff. The aim is to create a home-like environment and to give people as much independence as possible.

The local authority sets a weekly charge for its homes. This is the actual cost, but the amount people pay is based on what they can afford. People's income and other money is assessed and a price agreed. Where people are permanently resident in a home, any previous property owned has to be sold.

Voluntary organisations

Voluntary organisations are those which are independent of the government and not working to make a profit. They vary a great deal, and sometimes provide services for a particular group of people – perhaps those who have worked in a particular occupation, or people of a particular religion. There are often waiting lists. Some of these homes provide nursing care, and some are part of larger complexes including sheltered housing.

Private homes

There has been a huge boom in private care of elderly people. Evidence of this can be seen in popular retirement areas such as Clacton, in Essex. The increase in provision is partly a result of the increased number of elderly people. But an important boost to the private sector came in 1983 when the government changed the rules about benefits, allowing money to be paid for people to stay in private homes.

Many private homes are owned by individuals, some of whom have converted their own home to provide accommodation. Some are owned by larger companies. Standards vary enormously. Most private home-owners are caring people who provide excellent services, but some are simply looking for an easy way to make money. Scandals have been reported in newspapers, in which vulnerable elderly people have been exploited by uncaring owners.

The 1984 Registered Homes Act came into force in January 1985. This originally applied only to homes with three or more residents, although a change in mid-1992 has extended it to apply to all homes for elderly people.

An older person might welcome advice on what to take into a residential home

Private homes must be registered with the local authority. **Registration** means that the owner has to prove that he or she is a fit person to run a home. The facilities and staff must be adequate for the number of residents catered for. The home will continue to be inspected regularly after registration. If things are not as they should be, the **registration officer** can ask for changes to be made. Ultimately, the home can be closed down.

A code of practice for private home-owners was produced for the government by the Centre for Policy on Ageing. This gives guidelines on what rights older people should have in residential care. The booklet is called *Homelife*. It sets out a number of principles of care:

- the right to fulfilment;
- the right to dignity;
- the right to autonomy;
- the right to individuality;
- the right to esteem;
- the right to quality of experience;
- the right to take responsible risks.

The fees in private homes vary a great deal. Some homes are very luxurious and very expensive. As was mentioned earlier, the Department of Social Security will pay for less well-off people who need to be looked after in residential care. There are weekly limits to the amount the government will pay. These vary according to the amount of care needed by the elderly person. But the rates are quite low, and private home-owners find it difficult to provide good-quality care for the money. Some are prepared to take one or two residents with DSS funding, knowing that the money is not really covering the cost.

Finding out more: residential homes

★ Counsel and Care for the Elderly is an organisation which can provide advice and information for people thinking about moving into a residential or nursing home. Counsel and Care has lists of private and voluntary homes which are suitable for people in different circumstances and with particular needs. It also has contacts with charities who can provide money to top up Income Support to pay for care.

★ Age Concern produces an information sheet called *Finding Residential and Nursing Home Accommodation*. It is free, and can be obtained by sending a large stamped addressed envelope to Age Concern.

TO DO

1 Arrange to visit three residential homes – one provided by social services, one run by a voluntary organisation and one which is privately owned. (Make contact with the homes, and arrange times when it would be convenient to make these visits.)

2 Compare the facilities and the care provided. Find out the admission criteria and the weekly cost in each case. Does this cost include everything?

TO FIND OUT

Are there any homes specifically designed to meet the needs of people from ethnic minorities? One source for this information is the Central Council for Jewish Social Service. Local Community Relations Councils may also be able to provide information.

The future of residential care

Two trends are likely to continue into the future. The first is for people who might in the past have gone into residential care to stay in their own homes, or in some cases to stay there longer before moving into a residential home. There will therefore be more and more varied provision for people to be looked after at home. Many local authorities are beginning to employ people with titles such as 'community carers' to help people stay at home. Private and voluntary provision of this type is also growing.

The second trend concerns the question of who should provide residential homes for older people. *Community Care: agenda for action*, by Roy Griffiths (HMSO) – the Griffiths Report – was published in 1988. Several of its recommendations covered residential homes, which were seen as a part of the whole pattern of community care. The report recommended an increase in private and voluntary provision. The job of the local authority would be to monitor the independent sector. Griffiths thought it best if the local authority did not itself provide residential care, but instead bought it from these other organisations. He did recognise, however, that in some cases the local authority would have to be the provider. The report specifically mentions people 'with high dependency' and those with 'challenging behaviour'. In other words, where people are perhaps very confused, incontinent or violent, it would be best for the local authority to care for them.

The report also suggested that local authorities should set up independent inspection units for all kinds of residential care. It has sometimes irritated private home-owners that local authority homes do not have to meet the same standards set for private registration.

A year after the Griffiths Report had come out the government published a White Paper setting out its intentions for the law. This more or less echoed the Griffiths Report. In addition to the points described above, funding changes were to be introduced so that the money previously spent by the DSS on funding residents in private homes would transfer to local authorities. They would use it to purchase care for elderly people. If people were cared for in homes run by the local authority, the authority would continue to pay. This is a way of persuading the local authorities to use the independent sector instead of running their own homes for elderly people.

These ideas were included in the 1990 NHS and Community Care Act. The overall implication for the future is that fewer and fewer people will be cared for in local authority homes. Local authority homes are likely to take only people with particular needs.

WORDCHECK

sheltered housing A housing scheme which provides extra services, such as a warden.

service charge A payment made by occupants of sheltered housing to cover costs of services such as the warden and routine maintenance.

sinking fund A fund to cover major and unexpected expenses of sheltered housing, such as roof repairs.

Part III accommodation A term sometimes used to describe local authority provision for older people.

registration officer The person responsible for registering private- and voluntary-sector homes for older people and others.

TO DO

Consider the situation of a client who is an older person living in the community. (This can be a real person you work with or an imagined person, in which case you should describe the situation – housing, support and the like – and the personality, likes and dislikes of the person.) Imagine that the client is about to move into a residential home. How would you support him or her in this move?

- In visiting prospective homes, what would you look for? Compile a checklist of points which might indicate the quality of care offered.
- How could you help him or her to make the best use of a visit?
- Would a trial stay be helpful?
- What preparations would need to be made?
- How could links with the community be maintained?

TO FIND OUT

Contact the county council and find out about current plans for residential services for older people.

3 Health

The term **health care** tends to make people think of hospitals and surgeries, doctors and nurses. Yet most health care is provided not by professionals, but by relatives and friends. Relatives and friends are usually the first to be consulted when someone feels unwell. The doctors come second. A lot of basic nursing is not in fact done by nurses, but by untrained women in their roles as mothers, partners and daughters.

For some people, there may be no relatives or friends to turn to. This may be the case for an older person who is alone and isolated. Or for someone who has spent some time in a hospital – perhaps a psychiatric or mental-handicap hospital. Or for a young person who has come out of care, or who has had to leave his or her family. In these situations it may be the care worker who is asked for help. An elderly person may tell you that she needs dental care but does not feel able to get to the surgery. An adult with learning difficulties may not be happy with his doctor, and you may be the first to know about it. You may suspect that someone is worrying about her use of drugs or fears he has AIDS. In these situations it would be useful to know where to find information and whom to turn to.

This chapter provides information on various aspects of health care. The focus is on the various services which are available. Much of the health care we need is provided by the **National Health Service** (**NHS**). There are therefore sections describing the organisation of the health service and the various services within it. The NHS is dominated by one type of medicine, sometimes known as **Western medicine** or **orthodox medicine**. Some people choose **alternative treatments** and there is a section describing these, with suggested methods of finding further information. There is also a section describing ways of obtaining orthodox medical treatment outside the NHS.

As with everything else, health issues change. Diseases disappear, because of vaccinations or drugs or with changes in living standards. New health problems emerge. The most shocking and terrible in recent times was the discovery of the fatal effects of AIDS. Faced with a new problem large government organisations are slow to respond. It is often voluntary organisations which lead the field in meeting new needs. The Terence Higgins Trust is one such example. This organisation was established after the death of Terence Higgins, who died of AIDS in 1982. At that time there was very little information and support available. The Trust was set up by his friends to fill this gap. It has since grown very rapidly, and now meets many of the non-medical needs of people with HIV and AIDS.

In most areas of health there are voluntary organisations working. Often a given organisation is concerned specifically with one illness and provides special expertise in this area. Some organisations are self-help groups which allow people to talk with others who share the same problems and worries. This is especially important with illnesses which carry some kind of stigma, as do AIDS and mental illnesses.

The special needs of particular groups of people are increasingly being

Local voluntary groups help people with health problems. Cancerlink can provide information on starting a group to support people with cancer

A useful leaflet on health services for women

recognised. There are **Well Woman clinics** in many areas to provide preventive health care for women. In some areas there are **link services** within the NHS for people from ethnic minorities. A link worker will be based in a clinic or health centre and will aim to help overcome the language and cultural barriers between patients and doctors and nurses. Such workers are usually employed by health authorities in areas where a lot of Asian people live. There are also sources of information on particular diseases, such as sickle-cell anaemia which is more commonly found amongst people of African origin.

Finding out more: health-care provision

★   There is a vast number of voluntary organisations concerned with health. The following directories provide information on groups with addresses:

- *The Health Directory*, 1990. (London: Bedford Square Press.)
- *Voluntary Agencies*, 1989. (London: National Council for Voluntary Organisations.)
- *The Self-Help Guide: a directory of self-help organisations in the UK*, 1989. (London: Chapman & Hall.)
- *People Who Help*, 1990. (London: Profile Productions.)
- *Directory of British Organisations*, 1990. (CBD Research.)

These books are updated annually and are available in libraries. Health promotion departments would also have information on voluntary groups.

★   *Your Health, A Guide to Services for Women* is a free publication from the Department of Health. It can be obtained by writing to the Health Publications Unit.

★   Further information on issues related to black and Asian people can be obtained from the Commission for Racial Equality.

3.1 Advice and information on health care

For many people the first source of advice and information on health care is not an expert or a professional, nor a service set up to give specialist advice. People tend to turn first to those around them – relatives or friends. 'Do you think I should see a doctor?' 'Which dentist do you go to?' 'Do you know of a practice with a woman doctor?' 'How did you find a psychotherapist?' But some people do not have friends or relatives they can turn to. Some problems are too difficult, and need more specialised information. Sometimes people do not want to worry or frighten the people they love. Some illnesses – such as AIDS and mental illnesses – carry a stigma and people dare not ask for help from the people they know. This section describes the various sources of advice and information.

Some areas have **health information services**. These may be based in libraries, hospitals or health centres. They contain collections of books, articles and leaflets on all aspects of health. All health authorities have **health promotion departments**. (These used to be known as 'health education departments'.) In some areas they tend to focus on providing information for health-care workers, but some provide more of a public service. They

The Department of Health provides free information booklets

keep literature on health education (smoking, diet, exercise and the like) and information on local groups concerned with health issues. Each **District Health Authority (DHA)** has a **Community Health Council (CHC)**. This is made up of twelve members, whose job is to represent the local community in the health service. As well as being consulted in decision-making, they deal with complaints and provide information on local health services.

The media are also a source of information on health issues. Two examples are the BBC Radio 4 programmes *Does He Take Sugar?*, for people with disabilities, and *In Touch*, for people with a visual handicap. There are also frequent television documentaries on health problems and issues. Problem pages in newspapers and magazines are another popular source of information, especially on issues where people are afraid to ask anyone they know, including sometimes even their doctor.

Telephone **helplines** are becoming more common. There are commercial lines which provide taped information, but these are quite expensive – costing more than an ordinary long-distance call. Two examples are Healthcall and Bupa Medicall. There are also helplines which are free, for example the National Aids Helpline. Here the service offers information and advice for people worried about AIDS. It is not a pre-recorded service, but deals with individual enquiries. There are also local **Aidslines** in most areas, provided by the **Regional Health Authority (RHA)**. Many voluntary organisations specialising in particular conditions offer telephone helplines. One example is the Motor Neurone Disease Phoneline. There is also DIAL – Disablement Information and Advice Lines – which is run *by* people with disabilities *for* people with disabilities. There are over fifty groups throughout the country.

For most serious illnesses and conditions there is a voluntary organisation specialising in that area. Because these are so specialised, they are likely to know far more about the illness and the resources available to help than any general practitioner (GP) or general nurse could know. They can also provide the special understanding of people who have been in the same position. Often they offer to put people in touch with each other, to share

BACUP provides information for people with cancer

TO DO

1 Design a questionnaire to find out where people get information on health and health care.

- List as many sources as you can think of. Which of these have they used in the last six months? Include a category for 'Any other'.
- You might also like to find out whether people were happy with the information sources they used, and whether they would like more information to be offered.

2 Ask as many and as varied people as possible to complete your questionnaire.

3 If your results prove interesting you could send them to the local Community Health Council.

TO DO

1 Investigate sources of information in your local area.

- Is there a Health Information Service?
- Is there a local Aidsline?
- What services does the Health Promotion Department offer?
- Where is the nearest DIAL? (This can be found out from DIAL-UK.)

2 How can this information be made most accessible to your colleagues and your clients?

ideas and to provide mutual support. For example, there are two organisations which specialise in providing information on cancer. One is BACUP (the British Association of Cancer United Patients). The second is Cancerlink. Each provides a newsletter and information booklets with practical advice and information. BACUP has a telephone helpline staffed by nurses. Cancerlink supports local self-help groups with training and assistance.

WORDCHECK

Western or **orthodox medicine** The type of medicine practised in the NHS, which tends to emphasise the treatment of symptoms with drugs.

alternative or **complementary medicine** Forms of treatment other than Western or orthodox medicine.

stigma Something which sets a person apart and causes feelings of embarrassment or shame.

voluntary organisation An organisation which has not been set up by a government body and which does not aim to make a profit.

Well Woman clinics Clinics that provide preventive health checks for women.

link services Services provided by some health authorities to help people from ethnic minorities use the health service.

health information services Information services provided for the public by some health authorities, based perhaps in a hospital or health centre.

health promotion departments Services that provide information and health education.

District Health Authorities (DHAs) Organisations that manage the health service at the district level.

Community Health Councils (CHCs) Groups who represent the local community on health matters within the NHS.

helplines Telephone advice services.

Regional Health Authorities (RHAs) Organisations that manage the health service at a regional level.

Finding out more: health care

★ *The Health Care Consumer Guide* is an excellent guide to all aspects of health care, written by Robert Gann: it was published by Faber in 1991.

3.2 The organisation of the NHS

The NHS is a massive organisation. It is the largest employer in the UK. Not surprisingly, it has a complicated structure of management. This section describes the national structure of the health service.

Although most people use the health service reasonably successfully without understanding the overall structure, an overview can help in finding your way around the maze of different services and professionals. It can help also in understanding the major changes which are taking place in the health service.

These changes are a result of the 1990 NHS and Community Care Act. The key aspects of the Act are the creation of independent **NHS trusts** – hospitals and other units which opt out of the control of the District Health Authority – and the possibility for doctors in general practice to become **fund-holders**, spending their funds on hospital and other services.

1   Northern RHA
2   Yorkshire RHA
3   Trent RHA
4   East Anglian RHA
5   North West Thames RHA
6   North East Thames RHA
7   South East Thames RHA
8   South West Thames RHA
9   Wessex RHA
10 Oxford RHA
11 South Western RHA
12 West Midlands RHA
13 Mersey RHA
14 North Western RHA
15 Wales
16 Scotland
17 Northern Ireland

The organisation of the National Health Service

At the national level

The person ultimately responsible for the health service in Parliament is the Secretary of State for Health. He or she is the head of the **Department of Health Policy Board**, which is responsible for running the NHS in England. In Scotland, Wales and Northern Ireland there are separate Secretaries of State.

The Policy Board divides the money available for the NHS between the various regions of the country. There is also a board of directors of the NHS called the **NHS Management Committee**. This is in charge of the day-to-day running of the service.

At the regional level

England has fourteen **Regional Health Authorities** (**RHAs**) which plan services for their region. They give money to **District Health Authorities** (**DHAs**), **Family Health Service Authorities** and the GPs who manage their own funds. The new trusts – hospitals or other services which have opted out of health authority control – are responsible directly to the NHS Management Committee.

At the district level

Under the RHA are two organisations. The first is the Family Health Services Authority, which manages services provided by GPs, NHS dentists, chemists and opticians. The second is the District Health Authority. In England, there are 189 DHAs. Usually each is responsible for several hospitals – perhaps a district general hospital as well as several smaller ones – and the local clinics.

Hospitals

Within the health service there are now two types of hospital. The traditional hospitals are run by the District Health Authority. Under the NHS and Community Care Act, implemented in 1991, these must now compete to win contracts to treat patients, who are paid for by health authorities or fund-holding GPs. Secondly there are the NHS trust hospitals. These are hospitals which have opted out of the control of the health authorities. They get their money by competing to treat patients.

Outside the NHS there are also private hospitals, some of which are run by organisations for private health care, such as BUPA. People can pay personally, as individuals, or be paid for, through health insurance. Fund-holding GPs and District Health Authorities can buy services from private hospitals.

Doctors

Similarly, there are now two types of GP. *Fund-holding GPs* are financed directly from the Regional Health Authority. They can send patients to any hospital which seems to offer the best-value service. The bill is paid by the GP, unless it is over £5000 (April 1992), in which case the District Health Authority pays. *Non-fund-holding GPs* are funded by the District Health Authority. They can send patients to hospitals with which the DHA has a contract. If the treatment needed is not available at this hospital, patients can be sent elsewhere, so long as the DHA is prepared to pay.

WORDCHECK

NHS trusts Hospitals or groups of services which have opted out of the control of the health authority.

Department of Health Policy Board The national decision-making body for the NHS.

Secretary of State for Health The government minister responsible for the NHS.

NHS Management Committee The board of directors concerned with the day-to-day running of the NHS at a national level.

Regional Health Authorities (RHAs) Organisations that manage the health service at a regional level.

District Health Authorities (DHAs) Organisations that manage the health service at the district level.

Family Health Service Authorities Organisations that manage GP services.

fund-holding GPs General practitioners who have opted to control funds for their practice. These are used to buy services from hospitals and elsewhere.

Finding out more: the NHS

★ On 25 June 1991 the *Guardian* published a very useful three-page section on the NHS. Although this was printed in the section for schools, it would be useful for adults too. College libraries and some public libraries keep back copies of newspapers and make them available for reading and photocopying.

★ Information is available from the National Association of Health Authorities and Trusts and from the British Medical Association.

TO DO

Find out the local structure of the NHS.

- Which is the local Regional Health Authority?
- Which is the local District Health Authority?
- How are services managed by the DHA? They may be split into units covering different areas of health care.
- Have any local trusts been established? Are any in the process of being formed?
- Which doctors hold their own budgets?

This information should be available from the Regional or District Health Authority and from the Community Health Council. Address and phone numbers can be found in the *Yellow Pages* under 'Health authorities and services'.

3.3 The services provided by the NHS

There are many different professionals working in the health service providing a wide range of services. This section describes the main services. Within the NHS, these include:

- GPs;
- dentists;
- chemists;
- opticians;
- district nurses;
- health visitors;
- community psychiatric nurses;
- midwives;
- chiropodists;
- Well Woman clinics;
- hospitals;
- occupational therapists;
- physiotherapists;
- speech therapists.

There are also psychologists, psychiatrists and psychotherapists. (Services for people with mental illness are covered in a separate section.) Social workers work within the health service – in hospitals and with people with mental illnesses.

General practitioners (GPs)

GPs are independent and self-employed, but contracted to the health service through the Family Health Services Authority (FHSA). They are paid on the basis of the number of patients they have. Everyone has the right to register with a GP, and most of the services provided are free.

GPs are important as a means of access to other parts of the health service. They diagnose and treat everyday illnesses and conditions, but they also refer people to hospitals and other forms of more specialised care. Although some rural GPs still work alone, most are in group practices or health centres. A health centre will have a team of medical workers – usually including nurses, health visitors and midwives – as well as doctors. Increasingly, the teams are coming to include counsellors and social workers as well.

Everyone has the right to change their GP for any reason. Lists of local GPs are kept by the FHSA: these give details of the sex, qualifications and year of qualifying of each doctor. Details of surgery hours and the like are also listed. These lists are available from the FHSA or in libraries and Citizens' Advice Bureaux.

Finding out more: patients' rights

★ There is a leaflet called *Patients' Rights*. It is published by the Association of Community Health Councils, and is available in Welsh, Hindi, Punjabi, Gujarati, Urdu, Cantonese, Turkish, Vietnamese and Greek as well as English.

Dentists

In October 1990 a new contract for dentists came into force. People must now register with a dentist, as with a doctor. This involves signing on for *continuing care and treatment* for a period of two years. There is no cost involved in signing on. Dentists are paid for each continuing-care patient they have on their lists. Continuing-care patients are entitled to the full range of treatment available. They are entitled to free replacement or repair of most dental work if something goes wrong within a year. It is also possible to sign on as an *occasional patient*, for example if you need a dentist whilst on holiday. In this case you are not entitled to receive the full range of treatment.

Dentists must also, as a result of the new contracts, provide an information leaflet. This will explain how the practice works, including facilities for home visits and emergency treatment.

Dental treatment is not usually free. People have to pay for 75 per cent of the cost of all treatment, including examinations and X-rays. There is however a limit to the amount which can be paid for one course of

This leaflet, available from the General Dental Council, provides advice on dental care for older people

treatment, and some groups of people are **exempt** from payment. These are:

- all young people under 18;
- young people under 19 in full-time education;
- pregnant women;
- women with a baby under one year old;
- people on Income Support or Family Credit.

These people automatically get free treatment. Others on a low income can claim help with the costs.

Dentists must provide a treatment plan with details of costs. The patient does not have to decide immediately whether to go ahead, but can take this home for further thought.

Finding out more: dental care

★ For more information on help with dental costs, see the leaflet *NHS Dental Treatment* (leaflet D11) from the Department of Health. It is available from social security offices, doctors and dentists, and from the Health Publications Unit.

★ Age Concern produces a detailed and comprehensive leaflet with advice and information on dental care for elderly people. It is called *Dental Care in Retirement* and is free.

Chemists

Some drugs can be bought over the counter from any chemist. For others a prescription from a doctor is needed. As with dental treatments, prescriptions are not free. The charge is made per item. But again certain categories of people receive free prescriptions. These are:

- children under 16;
- students under 19 in full-time education;
- people on Income Support or Family Credit;
- people over retirement age;
- people on a war pension;
- pregnant women;
- women with a baby under 12 months of age;
- people on a low income.

People with certain long-lasting illnesses or conditions also receive free medication. These include diabetes and epilepsy.

People who do not qualify for exemption from payment but who need a lot of drugs can get a kind of **season ticket** for their prescriptions. These can be bought either for a four-month period or for one year. They are worth having if you are likely to need more than five items in four months, or more than fourteen items in one year.

Finding out more: prescription costs

★ For more information on free prescriptions, see the leaflet P11 *NHS Prescriptions* produced by the Department of Health. It is available from social security offices and doctors, and from the Health Publications Unit.

Opticians

Like dentists, opticians contract with the FHSA to provide services under the National Health Service. They test eyesight, write prescriptions for glasses, and sell glasses. Eye tests are free only to the following categories of people:

- children under 16;
- students under 19 in full-time education;
- people on Income Support or Family Credit;
- people who are registered blind or partially sighted;
- people over 40 who have a parent, brother or sister with glaucoma.

There is no set fee for an eye test, but it is likely to cost around £12 (April 1992). If glasses are needed, the optician will make out a prescription. This can be used to get glasses from that optician or any other.

NHS vouchers are available to help with the cost of the test and the glasses. People who automatically get a voucher are:

- people under 16;
- people between 16 and 19 and in full-time education;
- people on Family Credit or Income Support.

Others can claim help if on a low income. The vouchers are for varying amounts. They may be used in part-payment for glasses if someone wants to buy a more expensive pair. In some circumstances, people can qualify for contact lenses rather than glasses.

Finding out more: eye care

★   For more information on help with the costs of sight tests and glasses, see the Department of Health Booklet G11 *NHS Sight Tests and Vouchers for Glasses*. It should be available from social security offices, doctors and opticians, and directly from the Health Publications Unit.

District nurses

District nurses provide nursing care for people in their own homes. Their patients may be people who have been recently discharged from hospital, or people with disabilities who need nursing care and who would perhaps find it difficult to get to a health centre. Although district nurses may be attached to health centres they are employed by the health authority, not by the doctors. Often it is a doctor who arranges for a district nurse to visit a patient.

Health visitors

Health visitors are trained nurses, but the focus of their work is not on practical nursing. Rather they are concerned with health education. They mostly work with mothers of babies and young children, monitoring welfare and providing advice and support. Some health visitors work with older people or people with disabilities.

Community psychiatric nurses

These nurses provide support and counselling for people with mental illnesses who are living in the community. They also administer drugs. They may work through doctors or through a central mental-health centre. They see patients in the patients' own homes or at a centre. Some work with groups as well as individuals.

TO DO

Make a survey of the local opticians, looking for the best bargains. How much do they charge for a sight test? Compare the prices of spectacles at the opticians with those in other shops.

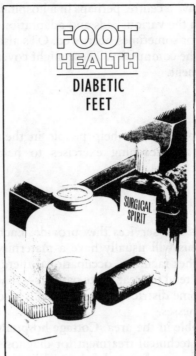

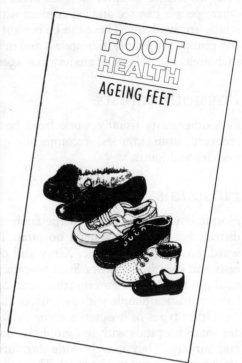

The Society of Chiropodists produces information leaflets on all kinds of foot care

Midwives

Midwives are often based in hospitals but some work in the community. They help pregnant women with antenatal care, deliver babies, and are involved in postnatal care when the baby has been born.

Chiropodists

Chiropodists work on problems people may have with their feet. Most people have to pay to see a chiropodist privately, but the following people are entitled to free treatment:

● women over 60;
● men over 65;
● schoolchildren;
● pregnant women;
● people with disabilities.

People may be referred by a doctor or they may contact a chiropodist themselves. There is often a waiting list for treatment. Chiropodists may visit older people in residential homes or at day centres.

Occupational therapists (OTs)

Some occupational therapists work within social services departments. Others are based in the health service, often working from hospitals. OTs are involved with the assessment of disability. They advise people with disabilities on how best to cope with the activities of daily living. Aids and adaptations can be recommended to make practical activities easier (for more on this see Chapter 5). Some areas have a centre, perhaps in a hospital, where people can see and experiment with the various aids and adaptations which are available. These can be bought or sometimes borrowed. OTs also run groups for people in hospitals and in the community. These might cover such areas as cookery or anxiety management.

Physiotherapists

Physiotherapists usually work from hospitals. They help people in their recovery from injuries, recommending and teaching exercises to help muscles and joints.

Hospitals

Hospitals vary in size and in the facilities and services they provide. Each district has a **district general hospital**. This will usually have a maternity ward, an out-patient clinic, X-ray and other facilities, occupational therapists and speech therapists. Such hospitals tend to treat **acute** patients – that is, those needing short-term treatment. Some district general hospitals also have wards for people with psychiatric illnesses.

Other types of hospital may be available in the area. **Cottage hospitals** are small hospitals with less emphasis on technical treatment for diagnosis and surgery. They may provide day surgery or be used for rehabilitation after a stay in a general hospital. There are also **day hospitals**, used for minor operations. Some areas have day hospitals for people with a mental illness.

Many towns have a large **psychiatric hospital**. In the past these hospitals provided long-term care for large numbers of people. Most also had acute wards. Over the last few years the numbers of people living in these hospitals have been reduced as patients have been moved out into the local community. Most such hospitals are scheduled for closure. The same applies to so-called 'mental-handicap hospitals' for people with learning difficulties. Increasingly people with learning difficulties are cared for in smaller units in the community.

WORDCHECK

district nurse Someone who provides nursing care in people's own homes.
health visitor Someone who provides health education, usually for families with small children or elderly people.
community psychiatric nurse Someone who provides support and nursing for people with mental-health problems who are living in the community.
Well Woman clinics Clinics that provide preventive health checks for women.
occupational therapist Someone who helps people with disabilities to live a normal life, teaching necessary skills and providing special equipment.
physiotherapist Someone who helps people with injuries, teaching them appropriate exercises.

TO DO

1 Find out what sort of hospitals there are in the local community.

- There will be a district general hospital. What facilities does it have?
- Is there a psychiatric hospital locally?
- Is there a day hospital? If you work with people who attend a day hospital, it might be possible to arrange a visit for yourself.
- Is there a local cottage hospital?

2 Consider these hospitals from your clients' points of view.

- How would they feel about entering these hospitals?
- How would you reassure them?
- Is there anything you could do to make a hospital visit easier?

TO DO

With the help of your supervisor, identify five clients of varying ages and circumstances.

- Consider each client's involvement with the health services.
- List the staff with whom the client is involved.
- What is the role of each of the health workers?
- Are there any gaps? Any unmet needs? Any areas of unnecessary overlap?
- Is the client happy with the service he or she is getting?
- Is there any way in which the client could get a better deal from the health service?

3.4 Special services for people who are terminally ill

People with terminal illnesses are likely to be using many of the NHS services described earlier in this chapter. However there are also specialised organisations which have been set up to meet the special needs of people with terminal illnesses. Two such services are described in this section.

Hospices

There are more than a hundred hospices in Britain. They provide care for people with terminal illnesses – often, but not always, people with cancer. They are often run by voluntary organisations and depend on donations from the public. There are also however hospices within the NHS.

Hospices aim to provide a style of care very different from that found in a hospital. Hospitals tend to be very busy places, full of hustle and bustle. They are orientated to curing patients. They are increasingly reliant on technology and are full of technical equipment for diagnosis and treatment. In contrast, hospices provide a calm and restful atmosphere. They are usually in attractive buildings with tranquil gardens and grounds. Nurses are never too busy to stop and listen. The aim is not to try to cure illnesses but to help patients to be as comfortable as possible. Hospices are very informal, with few rules and everything geared as far as possible to the needs of the individual patients.

Hospices have developed a system of preventive pain control. The philosophy is that there is no need for a patient to experience pain. Where hospital staff might administer drugs once pain is felt, the hospice method is to give the drugs before the pain starts. This is done by working out an individual programme of pain relief to help each patient. The same applies to other unpleasant symptoms of illness.

Hospice staff are involved in training other health-care professionals in their approach. Many hospices are also developing home-care facilities and day centres so that people can benefit from hospice methods whilst remaining at home.

TO DO

1 Find out whether there is a hospice near you. The Hospice Information Service has details of all the hospices. *The 1992 Directory of Hospices* is available free of charge and includes details of all the services available for people with terminal illnesses, at home and in hospices. A large stamped addressed envelope must be sent for a copy of the directory.

2 It may be possible to visit a local hospice. Some hold regular seminars at which they explain their methods of care. They are interested in helping others, such as workers in homes for older people, to develop the philosophy of care and the skills used in the hospice movement.

Macmillan nurses

Macmillan nurses work with people with cancer and with their relatives in the community. Initially each nurse is funded by a voluntary organisation called Cancer Relief, but it is expected that after three years the health service will take over the financing. There are over five hundred Macmillan nurses working in Britain. A few are based in hospitals but most work alongside GPs and other nurses in the community. They are specially trained, and provide emotional support as well as nursing care. Like the hospices, they specialise in pain and symptom control.

Cancer Relief also provides fourteen cancer-care units with in-patient wards, day-care centres and out-patient facilities.

Finding out more: Macmillan nurses

★ For information on Macmillan nurses and the other services it provides, contact Cancer Relief.

Macmillan nurses care for people at all stages of their illness, not just those with terminal cancer

3.5 Special services for people with HIV and AIDS

All the services which have been looked at in previous sections are available to people with **Human Immuno-deficiency Virus (HIV)** and those with **Acquired Immune Deficiency Syndrome (AIDS)**. There are however also some services which have been set up specially for these people. Many of these are provided by voluntary organisations, although some are provided by the health authorities. One positive outcome from AIDS is that it has encouraged a new kind of service delivery, in which people are very involved in the decision-making about their care and treatment.

Advice and information

There is a national **AIDS helpline** which keeps up-to-date information on all aspects of HIV and AIDS. Phone calls are free and the service can be used at any time. At certain times advice is given in Arabic and Asian languages. In most areas there is also a local **Aidsline**. The phone number may be found in the phone book.

Regional Health Authorities and District Health Authorities each have an AIDS and HIV co-ordinator. These people are often based in health promotion departments. They can provide advice and information on local and national services. The main organisation helping people with HIV and AIDS is the *Terence Higgins Trust*. This has grown very rapidly and now provides a wide range of services. One of the services is a telephone helpline staffed by trained counsellors who can offer advice, information and help. There are other voluntary organisations, too, all offering information and other services. For black and Asian people there is the *Black HIV and AIDS Network* and another organisation called *Blackliners*. There are organisations specifically for people with HIV; and *Positively Women* is for women with HIV or AIDS. The Terence Higgins Trust has a large library of books and videos on the non-medical aspects of AIDS. Anyone can make an appointment to use the library. Health promotion departments also keep libraries and the books can usually be borrowed.

Finding out more: HIV and AIDS

★   *Caring for Someone with AIDS* is an excellent guide to all the services a person with HIV or AIDS might need. It is published by Hodder & Stoughton. It was produced in 1990 by the Research Institute for Consumer Affairs and the Disabilities Study Unit, and edited by David Yelding. It includes services set up especially for people with HIV and AIDS, and also other services such as health services, benefits and legal services.
★   There are many free leaflets and booklets on HIV and AIDS. These can be obtained from health promotion departments or from the Health Information Line. No record is kept of people requesting information.

Support

The Terence Higgins Trust provides a number of different forms of support. One is the **buddy scheme**, which was first developed in the USA. Buddies work voluntarily and have training and support groups. They provide practical help and emotional support. Their aim is to help the person with AIDS to achieve the best possible quality of life and to remain as independent as possible. Other organisations also offer this type of service.

Most of the organisations involved with HIV and AIDS have set up support groups. These exist for people with HIV and AIDS and also for their families and partners. The Terence Higgins Trust also offers a counselling service. Some health authorities have set up **home-care teams** to help people with AIDS remain at home. The telephone helplines will be able to give information on the local availability of services.

Finding out more: voluntary organisations concerned with HIV and AIDS

★ All the voluntary organisations dealing with HIV and AIDS can supply information. The groups to write to are:

- The Terence Higgins Trust;
- Scottish Aids Monitor;
- Black HIV and AIDS Network;
- Blackliners;
- Positively Women.

Day centres in London

London has several day centres for people with AIDS. One is the London Lighthouse at 111/117 Lancaster Road, London W11 1QT. This offers a meeting place for people with AIDS. Partners, friends and families are also welcome. There are lounges and gardens. Services are available such as counselling and workshops on various issues. The London Lighthouse is open seven days a week.

Residential care

Hospices have been set up specifically for people with AIDS. One is the residential unit at the London Lighthouse. People can stay for short or long periods. It provides a pleasant and comfortable environment without the institutional features of a hospital. Anyone can apply for a place; admission will be considered on the basis of need.

The Mildmay Mission Hospital is a Christian charitable organisation but it cares for anyone in need. It has a homely atmosphere with single rooms and communal facilities. As with the London Lighthouse, people are accepted on the basis of need and urgency.

Finding out more: working with HIV and AIDS

★ There is a manual on all aspects of HIV and AIDS, prepared for organisations working in this area. It is updated regularly. It costs £195, or £55 for voluntary organisations. It is called the *National AIDS Manual*, and is available from NAM Publications Ltd.

TO THINK ABOUT

1 What support and guidance would you offer to someone who thought he or she might be HIV-positive?

2 Do you have any fears or prejudices which might make this difficult for you?

3 How could relatives or close friends be best supported?

WORDCHECK

hospices Residential centres which provide care for people who are dying.
Macmillan nurses A group of nurses who specialise in caring for people with cancer.
helplines Telephone advice services.
health promotion departments Services providing information and health education.
NHS trusts Hospitals or groups of services which have opted out of the control of the health authority.
buddy scheme A scheme that provides support for people with AIDS.

3.6 Special services for people with alcohol-related problems

Most people drink alcohol. Apart from the odd hangover, drinking is pleasurable and in most cases seems to do little damage. However, a minority of people drink excessively or inappropriately, and it is these people who are described as having **alcohol-related problems**. Alcohol is a poison which, in excess, causes damage to the liver and to other parts of the body, including the brain. Alcohol abuse also leads to problems at work and to arguments and breakdowns in family life. Alcoholics are psychologically and often physically dependent on alcohol.

Care workers have a threefold task in relation to alcohol-related problems. The first is one of prevention. This involves your being knowledgeable about sensible drinking and passing on this information to clients. It is perhaps especially important for young people to learn about alcohol, as habits are often formed early. Your second task is one of diagnosis. You need to be able to recognise the early-warning signs when drinking is becoming a problem. The third task is one of treatment and support. This may involve referral to one of the specialist agencies discussed later in this section.

Finding out more: alcohol-related problems

★   There are many leaflets and booklets on the subject of alcohol. These give advice on sensible drinking, provide guidance on recognising early stages of problem drinking, and give sources of information. There are leaflets and booklets specially geared to the needs of various groups, such as women, young people, older people and members of ethnic minorities. A useful guide to resources is *Breaking the Habit* by Iris Webb, produced by Thames Television. A readable general book on alcohol and health is *Alcohol: Our Favourite Drug*, by the Royal College of Psychiatrists.
★   The following are sources of information on alcohol and alcohol-related problems.

* The local health promotion department will hold a range of free leaflets; it will also have a library of books that may be borrowed.
* Triple A (Action on Alcohol Abuse) is a pressure group which aims to promote sensible drinking. It has an information journal and publishes various reports relating to alcohol.
* Alcohol Concern is a large national charity with government funding. It is involved in a wide range of activities, including running training courses, producing information, and supporting local groups and activities.
* DAWN (Drugs, Alcohol, Women, Nationally) produces information on all aspects of dependency for women.

Help for people with alcohol-related problems

Residential centres

There are various residential centres throughout the country. Some are private; some are run by voluntary organisations. The addresses can be found from Alcohol Concern or from local **alcohol advisory centres**. The centres work with various treatment programmes, often including group therapy.

TO THINK ABOUT

Do you have any stereotypes about alcoholics which might make it hard for you to recognise that someone has an alcohol problem? What mental picture is conjured up for you by the word 'alcoholic'?

The reality is that there are people with alcohol-related problems of all ages and in all walks of life. Women become alcoholics as well as men, for example, and Asians and Afro-Caribbeans as well as white people.

There are leaflets available which look at alcohol from a woman's point of view

Hospital treatment

Some NHS hospitals have **detoxification units,** in which patients are monitored in the days of withdrawal from alcohol. This is necessary only in very severe cases of alcohol dependence. (Detoxification can also take place at home with the support of a GP, a nurse and the family.)

The NHS also provides **alcohol treatment units** which offer an alcohol-free environment, social skills training, counselling and support. These may be for in-patients, out-patients or day patients.

Day centres

Day centres may be run by the health and social services or by voluntary organisations. *ACCEPT* is a national charity which runs day centres with counselling and other forms of therapy.

Self-help groups

Alcoholics Anonymous (AA) is the best-known self-help organisation. It has local groups in most parts of the country. It is a fellowship of recovering alcoholics. The philosophy of AA is one of total abstinence, and members follow a twelve-step plan to recovery. There is a religious aspect to this plan which can be off-putting to some. Although all groups follow the basic philosophy, each local group will have its own atmosphere: prospective members could usefully try two or three to find the one which best fits their needs. Anonymity is guaranteed in the AA.

AL-ANON family groups are a part of AA, providing support for the relatives and close friends of someone who is alcoholic or recovering from alcoholism.

ALATEEN is a part of AL-ANON run especially for teenage children of people with alcohol-related problems. People can join AL-ANON or ALATEEN even if the relative who abuses alcohol is not a member of the AA.

Drinkwatchers is a network of groups for people who are not dependent on alcohol but who want to cut down on their drinking.

Counselling

There are over forty **alcohol advice centres** (also known as **local councils on alcohol**) throughout the country. These provide specialist counselling and advice. The address can be found in the phone book or by contacting Alcohol Concern.

Finding out more: help with alcohol-related problems

★ The following organisations offer support:

- ACCEPT Clinic.
- Alcoholics Anonymous (AA): as well as the national office, there are local groups which can be found via the phone book;
- AL-ANON;
- ALATEEN;
- Drinkwatchers.

TO DO

Find out what sort of treatments and support are available locally. This will help you if you need to refer a client to a more specialist service.

- Is there an alcoholism treatment unit at the local hospital? Do patients attend as out-patients or in-patients? What kind of treatment is offered?
- Is there an alcohol advice centre (or a local council on alcohol)? What exactly is offered?
- Where is the nearest private clinic? If possible, visit and find out what the treatment programme is. Are there any other residential centres in the area?
- If possible, attend a meeting of the local AA group. What sort of people are at the meeting? What sort of atmosphere is there?

CASE STUDIES

Consider the following clients. What help, support and advice would be most appropriate for each?

(a) Bill is a man of seventy whose wife died some six months ago. Since her death his drinking has steadily increased. He is now asking his home help to buy in two bottles of whisky a week.

(b) Sarah is concerned about her seventeen-year-old son James who comes home drunk every Friday night.

(c) Pauline is a teacher in her thirties. Since the break-up of a relationship she has begun to rely on a drink in the evening. She drinks alone and before she goes out to see people. She has started to drink occasionally before school in the morning.

(d) Tom is twenty and lives on the streets since his mother threw him out of the house some eighteen months ago. He is drunk most days, usually on cider.

(e) Marcus is a successful businessman. He drinks with clients through the day and at home in the evening. He visits a health centre complaining of pains in his stomach.

3.7 Special services for drug and drug-related problems

Most health authorities have a department specialising in drug and drug-related problems. This will provide advice and information as well as counselling and treatment. Some also provide free **needle exchanges**. The department may or may not also work with people with alcohol problems.

Outside the health service, there is a national voluntary organisation which provides information on services for people with drug problems. This is *SCODA* – the *Standing Conference on Drug Abuse*. SCODA co-ordinates the work of voluntary organisations working in this area and provides a central source of information. It is also a pressure group, trying to influence the government and to improve the quality of services generally. Several publications are available from SCODA, including a newsletter and a directory of services, nationally and locally. SCODA also sets up meetings for people working in the field. Another voluntary organisation is *ADFAM National*. This provides advice and support for families and friends of people taking drugs. It has a telephone helpline. ADFAM also provides advice, information and training for people working with those with drug problems.

There are residential centres around the country which work to help people come off drugs. These usually have a structured programme of activities including group sessions and individual counselling. SCODA can provide information on these centres, with a brief summary of the approach in each case.

There is a national organisation specifically concerned with **solvent abuse** (or 'glue-sniffing'). This is called *Re-Solv*. Re-Solv has so far mainly worked to provide education and information for professionals who might come into contact with young people involved in glue-sniffing. It provides a newsletter and some useful publications. It also runs training sessions, helping people to learn to identify the signs of this problem. Currently Re-Solv is aiming to provide ways to help young people more directly.

Finding out more: help with drug-related problems

★ There are several self-help groups for people with drug problems. One is *Narcotics Anonymous*. A more specialised organisation is *TRANX*. This is specifically for people trying to stop taking minor tranquillisers, such as Valium. It offers advice and support. There is a telephone line and a drop-in service. TRANX will put people in touch with each other.

★ *ADFAM* is an advice and support service for families and friends of drug users. ADFAM also provides information for people working with drug users. *Families Anonymous* is a self-help group for relatives of people with drug problems.

Finding out more: working with drug users

★ *Drug Problems: where to get help* is a guide to services for drug users throughout the UK. It can be obtained from SCODA.
★ Two useful publications from Re-Solv are *Working with Solvent Sniffers: a guide for professionals* and the *Re-solv National Directory*. The first is by Richard Ives. The second is an excellent guide to national and local

services provided by the state and by voluntary organisations. Some are specifically concerned with glue-sniffing and some are more general.

WORDCHECK

alcohol advisory centres (also known as **local councils on alcohol**) Centres that provide counselling and information.

group therapy A way of exploring personal problems through discussion in a small group with a leader.

detoxification The monitoring of a person with severe alcohol dependency as the patient cuts out all alcohol.

alcohol treatment units NHS centres that help people with alcohol dependency.

needle exchange A place where drug addicts can exchange used syringes for new ones, to minimise the spread of infection.

TO DO

Consider the following clients:

- A woman who has been prescribed tranquillisers and sleeping tablets for some time and would like to stop taking these.
- A parent who suspects that her son is sniffing glue and other solvents.
- A young person addicted to heroin.

Imagine these people are your clients.

- Which national organisations would provide information?
- What local services could help?
- How could you help the clients make use of the services?
- What other support could you offer?

3.8   Help for people who are mentally ill

The GP is likely to be the first point of contact. He or she may be able to provide some counselling, although many GPs do not have the time or the training to offer this. In cases such as depression, GPs are likely to prescribe drugs, either anti-depressants or tranquillisers. The GP may want to refer the patient to a more specialised service.

Some areas have **mental-health centres**, which act as a kind of gateway for all mental-health services. These are multi-disciplinary, with a number of different workers based at the centre. These might include a psychiatrist, a psychologist, community psychiatric nurses and a social worker. There may also be art therapists and occupational therapists. In other cases, these services might be based at a hospital. In larger towns there may be mental-health centres working with people from particular ethnic backgrounds. Here the multi-disciplinary team may include a lawyer, to support people where there is an overlap between crime and mental health.

Finding out more: mental health

★   *Not on Your Own: the MIND guide to mental health* is written by Sally Burningham and published by Penguin (1989). It provides a clear and straightforward explanation of the various conditions. It also lists sources of help and gives practical advice on coping with mental illness.

★   MIND produces an excellent series of leaflets on the various mental illnesses. These explain the condition and the symptoms, look at possible causes, describe the various treatments and give sources of further information. The leaflets are:

- *Understanding Mental Illness*;
- *Understanding Manic Depression*;
- *Understanding Anxiety*;
- *Understanding Depression*;
- *Understanding Obsessions and Phobias*;
- *Understanding Schizophrenia*.

★   There are a number of organisations which provide information on particular mental illnesses. They may also have local groups and put people in touch with each other. The following are two examples:

- *Depressives Anonymous* provides a newsletter, meetings, pen-friends and advice on how to start a local group or information about an existing group.
- The *National Schizophrenia Fellowship* is for people with schizophrenia and also friends and relatives of people suffering from this illness. It provides information, advice and support. There are local groups which meet and sometimes are involved in local projects.

Mental-health professionals

A **psychiatrist** is a doctor who has specialist training in mental health. Some specialise further, perhaps in child psychiatry. People are usually referred to a psychiatrist through their GP. The psychiatrist makes an assessment. Following this, he or she may recommend admission to hospital, or that the patient sees another mental-health worker such as a psychotherapist for individual or group work. Psychiatrists also offer therapy themselves.

A **clinical psychologist** has a degree in psychology and has done further training. Clinical psychologists are involved in the assessment of mental-health problems. They also run groups and work with families and individuals.

Social workers help people with mental-health problems. They provide information and advice. They offer support for individuals and families. Some social workers have extra training in counselling and therapy, and work as therapists with individuals, couples or families. **Family therapy** is a specialised technique for untangling and resolving difficulties in whole families. Social workers also work with groups such as art groups, creative-writing groups and drama groups. They may offer groups for particular people, such as women, or girls who have experienced abuse. Some social services departments run drop-in centres. For people with long-term mental-health problems social services may run hostels, employment schemes and holidays.

Community psychiatric nurses (CPNs) also provide support and counselling for people in the community. They visit at home and work from mental-health or other centres. They can administer drugs.

Hospital care

The doctors and other health workers will try whenever possible to provide care for people with a mental illness in their own homes. Nowadays it is less common than in the past for people to be admitted to a hospital. Even patients who were admitted many years ago are being discharged into the community. However, there are still cases where hospital admission is necessary. Patients who need to go into hospital may go into a psychiatric ward of a district general hospital or into a psychiatric hospital. In a large psychiatric hospital there are usually different wards for different types of illnesses. There are acute wards for patients with short-term illnesses such as depression, and chronic wards for those with longer-term illnesses.

Hospitals provide various sorts of treatments. These include:

- drug treatments, from minor tranquillisers for cases of anxiety to major tranquillisers for problems such as schizophrenia;
- 'talking treatments', such as counselling, group therapy and psychotherapy;
- electro-convulsive therapy (ECT), for cases of very deep depression;
- behaviour modification – changing people's responses to situations, perhaps by systems of reward and punishment;
- psychosurgery (rarely used, and only as a last resort).

Large psychiatric hospitals have a variety of different staff. Day-to-day care is provided by psychiatric nurses. There are also psychiatrists, psychologists and social workers (see earlier). Occupational therapists also work in psychiatric hospitals, helping with rehabilitation. A hospital may also have special staff such as art therapists and drama therapists. These people work with patients, helping them to express their feelings.

Finding out more: mental-health treatments

★ MIND produces a set of pamphlets on some of the treatments for mental illnesses. These are called *Special Reports*. There is one available for each of the following treatments:

- major tranquillisers;
- minor tranquillisers;

- ECT;
- lithium treatment;
- anti-depressants.

The leaflets describe the treatment, as well as any possible side-effects.

Other sources of care

There are also services provided outside the NHS – by voluntary organisations, or privately. *MIND* (The National Association for Mental Health) is the main voluntary organisation concerned with mental health. At the national level, it campaigns to promote the rights of people with mental illnesses and to counter the stigma attached to mental illness. It produces a large number of excellent leaflets on various aspects of mental health. Further, it can provide legal and other advice from the national office. There are also some two hundred local MIND groups. The services provided vary from area to area, but may include drop-in centres, housing, social groups, employment projects and befriending schemes.

The *Samaritans* are another resource for people with mental-health problems. The Samaritans provide a confidential, 24-hours-a-day/7-days-a-week service. People can phone or visit the local office.

A different kind of listening and support is offered by **counsellors** and **psychotherapists**. Although counselling and psychotherapy are similar and overlap a great deal, there may be slight differences in emphasis. It is likely that a psychotherapist will concentrate on the client's past, especially their experiences as a child in the family. A counsellor will deal more with current problems and issues.

There are various different types of training which counsellors and psychotherapists may have had, but there are no legally required qualifications. The training consists of diplomas and master's degrees in counselling and psychotherapy, and suitably qualified people can apply for membership of the British Association for Counselling (BAC). Private therapy will cost £15–£30 for a 50-minute session. It is usually weekly and often long-term. It is not uncommon for people to see a therapist regularly for a year or more.

Sometimes it is possible to get therapy within the NHS, in which case it will be free. MIND may also provide a free counselling service locally. There may be other voluntary organisations which provide a counselling service, perhaps for particular groups such as young people or women. Another way to get free counselling or therapy is from students in training. It is worth contacting a local college to see whether this is possible.

Although counselling has something of a white middle-class image, it can help anyone who needs to talk through their problems. In some areas there are services specially tailored to the needs of people from ethnic minorities.

Finding out more: counselling and psychotherapy

★ There are several leaflets and many books which give information on counselling and psychotherapy.

- *Understanding Talking Therapies* is a leaflet produced by MIND in their series on mental illness (see above).
- *Counselling and Psychotherapy: is it for me?* is a leaflet produced by the British Association for Counselling.
- *A Complete Guide to Therapy* by Joel Koval, published by Penguin in 1978, explains the approaches of a number of different types of therapy.
- *Talking to a Stranger* by Lindsay Knight (Fontana, 1986).

★ For information on the names of counsellors and counselling and psychotherapy organisations, contact the British Association for Counselling. There is also the British Association for Psychotherapists. Another organisation involved in therapy, for women only, is the Women's Therapy Centre.

Therapeutic communities

Around the country, there are a number of therapeutic communities run by voluntary organisations. One example is the communities run by the *Richmond Fellowship*. The communities provide a supportive environment in which people help each other, with back-up provided by trained staff. There will usually be group meetings to discuss day-to-day decisions and to allow people to talk through their feelings and problems. State funding may be available for someone who would benefit from this kind of support. Information on therapeutic communities is available from MIND.

Finally, there may be day centres, drop-in centres and various groups provided by people with mental illnesses. These may be run by social services departments or by a local MIND group.

WORDCHECK

mental-health centres Gateways for people with mental-health problems who are seeking help.
psychiatrist A doctor who specialises in mental health.
psychologist Someone with a degree in psychology, involved usually in assessment.
community psychiatric nurse Someone who provides support and nursing for people with mental-health problems who are living in the community.
occupational therapist Someone who helps people with disabilities to live a normal life, teaching necessary skills and providing special equipment.
family therapy A way of exploring relationships and problems between members of a family, all of whom are involved in the therapy.
acute ward A short-stay ward in a hospital.
chronic ward A longer-stay ward in a hospital.
group therapy A way of exploring personal problems through discussion in a small group with a leader.
electro-convulsive therapy (ECT) Treatment for severe depression which involves passing an electric current through the brain.
behaviour modification Treatment to change behaviour: it involves systems of reward and punishment.
psychosurgery Treatment for severe mental illness, very rarely used, which involves surgery on the brain.
stigma Something which sets a person apart and causes feelings of embarrassment or shame.
voluntary organisation An organisation which has not been set up by a government body and which does not aim to make a profit.
therapeutic community A residential centre which can help people come to terms with their feelings and solve emotional and psychological problems.

Finding out more: therapeutic communities

★ The Richmond Fellowship can provide information on the therapeutic communities it runs.
★ Another source of information on therapeutic communities is *A Directory of Therapeutic Communities*, available from the Association of Therapeutic Communities.

TO DO

Consider the following clients. Which services, nationally and locally, would be able to offer some help?

(a) Charlene, a mother of small children, who is suffering from depression.

(b) Curtis, a man diagnosed as schizophrenic some thirty years ago, who has spent many years in hospital but currently lives in a flat in the community.

(c) Muhammed, a young man who has recently started his first year at university, who is withdrawn and unable to work.

(d) George, a man of 70 who has not left the house and has barely spoken since the death of his wife a year ago.

The law and mental illness

This mostly concerns hospitalisation of people with a mental illness. By far the majority of people with a mental illness who are in hospital are there as **informal patients**. This means that they have gone into hospital voluntarily. They have the same legal rights as someone in hospital for treatment for a physical illness. Informal patients can leave the hospital if they want to, and they do not have to accept treatment. About 95 per cent of patients in psychiatric hospitals are informal patients. The remaining 5 per cent of **formal patients** are in hospital under one or other section of the 1983 Mental Health Act. They cannot leave when they please, and they have lost some other rights as well.

There are four sections of the Mental Health Act which are especially relevant when people are so mentally ill that it is necessary to admit them compulsorily to hospital. This may be done because it is thought that they are a danger to themselves – that they are likely to try to commit suicide or in some other way harm themselves. Sometimes mentally ill people become violent and are a danger to others. Such people may not consider themselves to be mentally ill, and may refuse any help or treatment. This section explains how the law can be used in such cases. The law on mental health is powerful since it gives social workers and doctors the right to take away people's freedom and to force people to go into psychiatric hospitals. It is important that it is not abused. There is a safeguard with the **Mental Health Review Tribunal** (**MHRT**) which allows patients to have their cases reviewed.

Section 4

Section 4 of the Mental Health Act is concerned with admission to hospital in emergency cases. The application for admission is made by a social worker or a close relative. The social worker must be an **approved social worker** (**ASW**), who has completed extra training in this area of work. The social worker or relative must have seen the person in the last 24 hours. Then it is necessary for a doctor to agree that there is an 'urgent necessity' for the patient to be admitted and that to wait would cause 'undesirable delay'.

Admission is for 72 hours only. At the end of that period, the patient may stay in hospital as an informal patient. Alternatively, the patient may leave, unless the doctor decides to keep the patient in hospital under a longer section.

Section 2

Under Section 2 of the Mental Health Act a patient can be admitted to hospital for a maximum of 28 days. Again the application must be made by an approved social worker or the nearest relative. The social worker or relative must have seen the patient in the last 14 days. Two doctors must agree that the person needs to be in hospital and is otherwise a danger to himself or herself or to someone else. The patient can apply to a Mental Health Review Tribunal within 14 days of being admitted, as a means of having the case reviewed.

In certain cases, the patient may leave hospital before the 28 days are up. This can happen if someone is discharged by their doctor, or by the hospital management or the MHRT. The nearest relative can also discharge the patient, but must give 72 hours' notice to the hospital. If the doctor does not agree with the patient leaving, the doctor can overrule the relative.

At the end of the 28 days, the patient can leave, or stay as an informal patient, or be kept in the hospital for a longer period under another section of the Mental Health Act.

Section 3

Section 3 of the Act allows a person to be kept in hospital for six months in the first instance. This can be extended for a further six months. After that, the extensions are for one year at a time. Two doctors must agree that hospitalisation is necessary in the interests of the safety of the individual or of others. Patients can apply to the MHRT once in the first six months and once in the second six months. After that the case is reviewed annually.

Section 5

Section 5 of the Act is concerned with people already in hospital as informal patients. A doctor can prevent an informal patient from leaving the hospital for 72 hours by telling the hospital management that an application for a section should be made. A nurse can keep someone in hospital for up to six hours or until the arrival of a doctor with the authority to keep the patient.

Representation at a tribunal

Patients are allowed to have someone else to represent them at a Mental Health Review Tribunal. This can be anyone, but it is best to have someone who understands and can use the law on mental health. Both MIND and the Law Society can recommend someone with special expertise in this area. If a solicitor is used, a patient with a low income can have free representation under the legal aid scheme.

WORDCHECK

informal patient A patient who is in hospital voluntarily and not under any part of the mental-health legislation.
Mental Health Review Tribunal A body which reviews cases of people admitted to psychiatric hospitals under the 1983 Mental Health Act.
approved social worker A social worker with extra training who is involved with admitting people to psychiatric hospitals.

Finding out more: mental health and the law

★ MIND produces two useful leaflets on the law and mental health. These are:

* *The Mental Health Act 1983 – an outline guide*;
* *Mental Health Review Tribunals.*

★ See also *Law for Social Workers* by Hugh Brayne and Gerry Martin, published by Blackstone Press in 1990.

CASE STUDY

Janet is a single parent with a four-year-old son. Over the last six months her behaviour has become increasingly bizarre and erratic. Previously a good mother to her son, she is now confusing him with her strange behaviour. Her relatives are concerned for her welfare and for the little boy. The relatives contacted social services but Janet would not open the door to the social worker on his second visit.

1 How could the law be used in this example? Which are the relevant sections? Which professionals need to be involved?

2 Apart from using the law, how else could Janet be helped? What treatments might be appropriate? Which mental-health workers could get involved? Which other services might be needed?

Publications from MIND
Spring 1992

MIND produces leaflets on all aspects of mental illness

3.9 Private health care

Some people choose to pay for private health care. It may be that they feel they will receive a better standard of care than they would get in the NHS. The differences tend not to be in the quality of medical care received, however, but in the 'frills' – the availability of private rooms, telephones, and so on. Another reason people choose private health care is that there are long waiting lists in the NHS for certain – usually, but not always, non-urgent – types of treatment. One example here is hip-replacement operations: 28 per cent of these are carried out privately.

There are now about two hundred private hospitals around the country and about three thousand 'pay beds' in NHS hospitals. The majority of people paying privately do so through one or another of the private insurance companies. Two of the largest are *British United Provident Association* (BUPA) and *Private Patient Plan* (PPA). About two million people subscribe to private insurance schemes. Since a lot of subscriptions are for families, this means that about six million people have private cover.

There are limits on what private insurance will cover. Some companies will not take people over 65 as new subscribers, for example. Someone with a disability or long-standing illness can join, but he or she will not be insured for any treatment of an illness they had at the time of joining. This also applies to any condition *related* to an existing illness. Likely exclusions include:

- seeing a GP privately;
- routine health checks;
- out-patient drugs;
- cosmetic treatments;
- convalescence;
- maternity care;
- items such as glasses or wheelchairs;
- routine dental work;
- any HIV-related treatment within (say) five years of joining.

There are also limits to the amount which can be claimed. Private health insurance works best for basically well people who might need minor treatment for an acute short-term illness or injury.

Finding out more: private health care

★ For more information on private health care, contact The Medical Advisory Service. This organisation can give information on all health resources, not just private ones.

TO DO

Contact at least two private health insurance schemes. Find out the costs.

Look carefully at the small print to see exactly what cover is given and what is excluded. Compare the two schemes, and make notes on their strengths and weaknesses.

3.10 Alternative medicine

The kind of medicine offered within the NHS is only one approach to medicine. It tends to concentrate on physical symptoms and to rely heavily on drugs and surgery to treat symptoms. Some people are not happy with this approach or have found it ineffective for a particular illness or condition. Alternative approaches do exist. There are many types of **alternative medicine** but the most common alternative practitioners are osteopaths, homeopaths, acupuncturists, chiropractors and herbalists. Sometimes these approaches are known as **complementary medicine**, as many people use them in addition to rather than instead of conventional medicine. This section looks at the commonest types of alternative medicine.

Acupuncture

Acupuncture is an ancient Chinese art. It involves needles being placed in particular parts of the body. The needles may be left for seconds only or for a longer period such as half an hour. The needles may have electricity passed through them or they may be manipulated by hand. Although it sounds as if it must be painful, users say it is not.

Finding out more: acupuncture

★   The British Medical Acupuncture Society has a list of members who are not conventional doctors and who also practise acupuncture. People seeking treatment must be referred by their own GP.

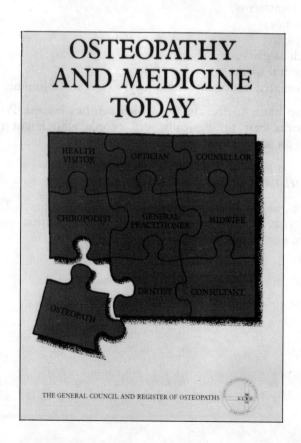

The General Council and Register of Osteopaths has information leaflets on osteopathy

★ The British Acupuncture Association has members who are not conventionally qualified doctors.

Osteopathy

Osteopathy is the most popular type of alternative treatment in the UK. Osteopaths take a holistic approach, looking at the whole person: their personality and lifestyle, as well as symptoms such as pain. The treatment involves physical manipulation of the spine and joints.

Finding out more: osteopathy

★ The General Council and Register of Osteopaths can provide information.

Chiropractic

This is similar to osteopathy. It is gaining in popularity and in other parts of the world is more commonly practised than osteopathy. Like osteopathy, it involves physical manipulation of the back and limbs. Chiropractors are more likely to use more sudden thrusting movements, whereas osteopaths combine their treatment with massage.

Finding out more: chiropractic

★ The British Chiropractors' Association can provide information.

Homeopathy

This is another holistic approach to medicine. The homeopath will spend a relatively long time finding out about the patient. Life history, personality and lifestyle will be taken into account in making a decision on the best treatment. There are two main principles in homeopathy. The first is that like can cure like, and that the smallest dose of a treatment is the most effective. Secondly, symptoms are seen positively: as part of the body's attempt to cure itself. Homeopaths do not treat people with infectious diseases or injuries or cancer – they are most popular in treating conditions such as allergies, pains in joints, and stomach problems.

Some doctors who practise within the NHS have also trained in one of the alternative treatments. These doctors may be able to offer treatment within the NHS. Homeopathy can be obtained within the health service and there are hospitals working to these principles which can take NHS patients. Homeopathic medicines can be bought at chemists and health shops.

WORDCHECK

alternative or **complementary medicine** Forms of treatment other than Western or orthodox medicine.
osteopath Someone who treats injuries by manipulating the spine and joints.
homeopath Someone who practises alternative healing, by treating the whole person with small doses of medicine.
acupuncturist Someone who treats people by inserting needles into the body.
chiropractor Someone who treats injuries by manipulation of the back and limbs.

HOMOEOPATHY

Your Questions Answered

British Homoeopathic Association
27A Devonshire Street
London W1N 1RJ
Telephone 071-935 2163

The British Homoeopathic Association provides information on homeopathy

Finding out more: homeopathy

★   The British Medical Homeopathic Association has members who are trained as orthodox doctors and who also practise homeopathic medicine.
★   The Society of Homœopaths has members who are not conventional doctors.

Choosing a practitioner

There is no law controlling alternative medical practice. Anyone, without any qualifications, can set themselves up as a healer. So prospective patients need to be cautious. It is worth checking that the practitioner is registered with the appropriate professional body and has training and qualifications.

Finding out more: alternative medicine

★   *The Handbook of Complementary Medicine* by Stephen Fulder (Oxford University Press: 2nd edition, 1988) gives detailed information on all alternative forms of treatment. It also has references for further information.
★   Penguin publishes a guide called *Alternative Medicine*, by Andrew Stanway (1982). Penguin also publishes a series of books, one on each of the main forms of alternative medicine.
★   The Institute for Complementary Medicine provides information on a wide range of alternative treatments.

TO DO

1   Find out about practitioners of alternative medicine in your area. The phone book is a useful source of information, or the organisations listed could be used.

2   Conduct a survey to find out how many people have consulted an alternative practitioner. Without being too personal, try to find out their reasons for doing so. Were they happy with the treatment? Would they recommend the healer?

4 Money

This chapter looks at ways in which people are entitled to financial help. This is an important area of need as money is the means to so much in life. Poverty affects physical health and reduces people's opportunities.

Most of the information in this chapter concerns social security benefits. The system is complicated and no one – probably not even the people who work in the social security offices – could be expected to know everything about all the benefits. But it is important that people in the caring professions have at least an *outline* knowledge of what people can claim, and certainly that they know how to find out what is available.

Millions of pounds of benefits go unclaimed each year. One of the main reasons for this is ignorance. People are not aware that the benefits exist, or that they would be eligible for a benefit. This is where you can help, by tactfully finding out whether your clients are receiving all the benefits they are entitled to. Another reason people do not claim benefits is that they are frightened of all the form-filling and the questions they might have to answer. Your support might be welcomed. It is not necessary to be an expert to accompany someone to the benefit office or to help with filling in a form. Some people, especially older people, feel that benefits are a form of charity and they would feel ashamed to claim. They need convincing that the welfare benefits are their right. They have paid into the system through taxes and national insurance. Even someone who has not paid tax through work will have paid tax on things they have bought.

Social security benefits: some general principles

As has been mentioned, the bulk of this chapter is concerned with social security benefits. It is mainly divided in terms of various types of people and the benefits they might be entitled to. However, there are some benefits which people can get in many different situations. These are described first and then referred to throughout the later sections.

In understanding the benefits system, a few general principles will help. Firstly, benefits are divided into those which are means-tested and those which are not. When a **means-tested benefit** is claimed, the income and savings of the person will be looked at. Only people who have incomes and savings below levels set qualify for the benefit. The main benefits which are means-tested are Income Support, Housing Benefit and Family Credit.

Secondly, some benefits are **contributory**. This means that only people who have paid the right amount of national insurance contributions will be able to claim the benefit. Many people think that everyone gets the retirement pension, but this is not so. It is only paid to people who have qualified through their own or their husband's contributions whilst in work. The contributory benefits include the retirement pension, unemployment benefit and the widows' benefits. Statutory sick pay and statutory maternity pay are also contributory.

Some benefits, however, are neither means-tested nor contributory. This is the case with Child Benefit and One-Parent Benefit. Child Benefit is paid to all families with children. One-Parent Benefit can be claimed by all lone parents. (In practice, One-Parent Benefit is only helpful to working parents, since it counts as income in assessing Income Support, and the amount of Income Support paid will therefore be reduced.)

Most benefits are paid according to rules which have been set by Parliament. A few benefits, however, are **discretionary**. This means that the officers assess the claimant's case and decide whether or not the benefit should be given. This is the case for some of the payments from the Social Fund.

The rates at which benefits are paid change each April, and occasionally at other times too. This presents a problem when writing about benefits. In describing the benefits I have, in the main, left out the actual amounts, since these will have changed by the time this book is published. An exception to this is in the examples. Here I wanted to show the kinds of payments which can be expected. The amounts shown relate to the year 1992–93. They can be updated by reference to the sources given below.

Advice on benefits

Some local authorities provide a **welfare rights unit** to help people with advice and information on benefits. There may also be a local **law centre** which offers free legal and welfare advice. All areas have **Citizens' Advice Bureaux** (CABs) which give free advice in this area. Sometimes the CAB will help with appeals on benefits. There may also be a local *Child Poverty Action Group*. **Claimants Unions** have been set up in some areas: information about these is available from the Federation of Claimants Unions. There are free help lines for general benefits advice run by the DSS.

Finding out more: benefits

★ The Child Poverty Action Group produces two excellent and detailed guides to benefits. These are updated each April, when the majority of changes are made to the benefits system. The books are:

- *National Welfare Benefits Handbook*;
- *Rights Guide to Non-Means-Tested Benefits*.

★ The Department of Social Security produces a large number of leaflets explaining the various benefits. These are very well produced and most are easy to understand. They range from brief leaflets which give an outline of benefits – to help people find out whether the benefit is worth claiming – to very detailed and comprehensive booklets containing all the rules concerning a benefit. The leaflets are free and are available in DSS offices, libraries and post offices. Or they can be obtained by writing to the DSS Information Division (Leaflets Unit).

The DSS booklets are well produced and easy to understand

WORDCHECK

means-tested benefit A benefit awarded to some and not to others, according to the individual client's income and savings.

contributory benefit A benefit payable to someone who has paid enough national insurance contributions.

discretionary benefit A benefit awarded to some and not to others, the decision being taken by an official according to the merits of the individual case.

law centre A centre which provides free legal advice.

4.1 Income Support

Income Support is one of the key benefits in the social security system. It is paid to people in a variety of different situations. The common factors are that people who receive Income Support are not working full-time (that is, more than 16 hours a week) and that they have an income which is below a level set by Parliament. The levels for people of different ages and in different situations are explained below.

Entitlement

People on Income Support may have no other income at all, or they may have income from maintenance or other benefits or from a part-time job. In most cases, other income is taken into account in deciding how much benefit will be paid. Another qualification for Income Support concerns savings. People cannot claim Income Support if they have more than £8000 (April 1992) in savings. People with savings, but less than this amount, will find that their benefit is reduced (see below).

The amount of Income Support a person will get is worked out by looking at any income coming in and comparing this to the amount Parliament has decided people are entitled to, known as the **applicable amount**. The amount paid is the balance between these two amounts of money.

Income Support = applicable amount – income

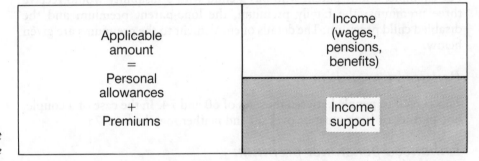

As mentioned above, people with savings over £8000 (April 1992) cannot receive Income Support. People with savings between £3000 and £8000 will have some money deducted from the benefit: the deduction is £1 each week for every £250 or part of £250. If the benefit officers suspect that someone has deliberately got rid of their savings in order to claim benefit, this person can be treated as if he or she still has the savings.

Income is counted *after* tax and national insurance deductions. Pensions and earnings count as income, as do certain social security benefits: Child Benefit, for example, is counted in calculating Income Support. Not all income is counted, however. The following are ignored:

- Attendance Allowance;
- Mobility Allowance;
- Social Fund payments;
- interest from savings;
- expenses from voluntary work;
- £5 from earnings, or £15 if the person is a lone parent or has a disability;
- £4 from rent paid by a sub-tenant.

Allowances and premiums

As shown in the diagram on page 61, there are two parts to the amount of money decided by Parliament. These are the **personal allowances**, which are based on the number and ages of people in the family; and the **premiums**, which are based on certain aspects of the person's situation. The premiums are supposed to reflect special needs and additional expenses. A personal allowance is paid for each member of the household (a couple receive a different amount). The rates vary according to age.

Premiums are paid *on top of* the personal allowances. There are nine different premiums. Each person may receive *one only* of the following:

- pensioner premium;
- enhanced pensioner premium;
- disability premium;
- higher pensioner premium;
- lone-parent premium.

If someone is eligible for more than one, he or she will receive the *higher* premium only.

One or more of the following premiums may be received *as well*, however:

- carer premium;
- family premium;
- disabled child premium;
- severe disability premium.

For example, a lone parent who has a child with a disability would receive three premiums: the family premium, the lone-parent premium and the disabled child premium. The details of entitlement to the premiums are given below.

Pensioner premium

This is paid to people between the ages of 60 and 74. In the case of a couple, one partner or both must be over 60 and neither may be over 75.

Enhanced pensioner premium

This is paid to people between the ages of 75 and 79. For a couple to qualify, one must be aged over 75 and neither may be over 80.

Disability premium

This is paid to people under 60 who receive one of the following benefits:

- Attendance Allowance;
- Mobility Allowance;
- Invalidity Pension;
- Severe Disablement Allowance.

It is also paid to people who are registered blind, or who have a DSS-registered invalid carriage. A couple will get the premium if one or both of them qualify.

Higher pensioner premium

This is paid to people aged 80 and over; and to people between 60 and 79 who have a disability.

Lone-parent premium

This is paid to men or women who are caring for a child and who have no partner.

Carer premium

This is for people caring for another person, who receives the Invalid Care Allowance. Others can receive the premium if they would qualify for the Invalid Care Allowance were it not for another benefit they are getting instead.

Family premium

All families with dependent children receive this premium. This includes lone parents, who therefore receive two premiums.

Disabled child premium

This is paid for each child who receives the Attendance Allowance or the Mobility Allowance, or who is registered blind.

Severe disability premium

People qualify for this if they are receiving the Attendance Allowance, live alone, have no one caring for them, *and* receive the Invalid Care Allowance. There is a single rate for couples when both receive the Attendance Allowance and when a carer receives an Invalid Care Allowance for one of them. The double rate is paid if neither has a carer receiving the Invalid Care Allowance and if both receive the Attendance Allowance.

4.2 Young people and Income Support

Since September 1988, 16- and 17-year-olds have not been able to claim Income Support. The idea is that they should be in full-time education, in work or on a training scheme. This caused great hardship for some young people and led to the increase in homeless young people begging on the streets of towns such as London.

Some exceptions to the rule that people must be 18 to claim Income Support have been introduced. In some circumstances, young people are entitled to claim for a short period of time, provided they are registered for a job or a place on a training scheme. This is known as the child **benefit extension period**. The 'special circumstances' apply if the person:

- is married;
- has no living parent or guardian;
- was living away from home and in care or custody immediately before the age of 16;
- is placed away from home on a rehabilitation programme by a social worker;
- is living away from home to avoid abuse;
- is away from home because of a mental or physical disability;
- has parents in prison, or who are chronically sick or mentally disabled;
- is away from home because estranged from his or her parents, or in physical or moral danger, or at risk to his or her physical or mental health.

There are other circumstances in which a young person may be eligible for benefit at any time. These affect:

- couples (married or unmarried) responsible for a child;
- lone parents;
- people with disabilities who are incapable of work or training;
- others who are caring for a child or disabled adult;
- blind people;
- pregnant young women, from 11 weeks before the baby is due;
- people who are temporarily sick or disabled.

Finally, the Secretary of State for Social Security has the discretion to allow Income Support to be paid to prevent 'severe hardship'. This tends only to be for a short period of time. People seeking emergency accommodation in shelters are automatically considered under this rule.

WORDCHECK

Social Fund A fund which can provide loans and grants for buying larger items or in times of crisis.

premium A part of Income Support, for people with extra needs such as older people or one-parent families.

personal allowance The other part of Income Support, calculated on the basis of age.

There are some situations in which young people can claim Income Support. This leaflet explains

Who gets Income Support?

The following people are entitled to Income Support:

- an older person whose pension does not bring him or her up to the level of Income Support for someone in that situation;
- an unemployed person who has not paid enough national insurance contributions to receive Unemployment Benefit;
- an unemployed person who receives Unemployment Benefit but who is still below the amount of money for Income Support (this would be the case for most people with children);
- a lone parent, not working;
- a lone parent, working part-time, whose income is low enough still to qualify for Income Support.

EXAMPLE 1

Jaswinder has just finished studying at a polytechnic. She is 21 and not able to find work straightaway. She qualifies for Income Support. She receives:

Eligibility

Personal allowance	£33.60
Premiums: none	£ 0.00
	→ £33.60

Deductions

None	£ 0.00
	→ £ 0.00
Income Support paid:	£33.60

This money will have to cover everything except rent and 80 per cent of Jaswinder's Community Charge. The rent will be paid with Housing Benefit (section 4.4).

EXAMPLE 2

Jane is a lone parent with a daughter, Olivia, aged 4. Jane herself is 28. They live in a rented house and Jane has no income other than Child Benefit. She is eligible for Income Support. She receives:

Eligibility

Personal allowance:	
Jane	£42.45
Olivia	£14.55
Premiums:	
family	£ 9.30
lone-parent	£ 4.75
	→ £71.05

The Child Benefit and One-Parent Benefit count as income and are taken off the amount to be paid as Income Support.

Deductions

Child Benefit	£ 9.65
One-Parent Benefit	£ 5.85
	→ £15.50
Income Support paid:	£55.55

Jane's total income will therefore be £71.05 (the Income Support plus the two benefits), which will have to cover everything for Olivia and herself except rent and 80 per cent of Community Charge.

EXAMPLE 3

John is unemployed. He has been unemployed for two years, so his Unemployment Benefit has finished. He has four children: Jim aged 14, Sally aged 10, and twins Sam and Jo aged 5. His wife Mary works part-time and earns £15. The applicable amounts for the family are:

Eligibility

Personal allowance:		
John and Mary	£66.60	
Jim	£21.40	
Sally	£14.55	
Sam	£14.55	
Jo	£14.55	
Premiums:		
family	£ 9.30	
	└───→	£140.95

The income to be counted is the Child Benefit and all except the first £5 of Mary's wages.

Deductions

Child Benefit	£ 9.65	
	£ 7.80	
	£ 7.80	
	£ 7.80	
Earnings less £5.00	£10.00	
	└───→	£43.05
Income Support paid:		£97.90

The Family's total income will be £140.95 (Income Support plus Child Benefit and earnings). In addition they may qualify for Housing Benefit: this would be all of the rent if they rent a house, or the interest on a mortgage if they own one.

4.3 The Social Fund

The Social Fund is meant to help people with larger and exceptional payments – the kind it is hard to plan for and which cannot be paid for out of weekly benefit payments. There are two parts to the Social Fund, making *discretionary* and *non-discretionary* payments.

The **non-discretionary payments** are made according to rules set down in law: people receive the payment if they meet the criteria. They receive a set amount decided by Parliament. This type of payment is made for funerals and for maternity costs. Cold Weather Payments are also made on a non-discretionary basis.

The **discretionary payments** are of three types: Community Care Grants, Budgeting Loans and Crisis Loans. With these, each case is assessed by a Social Fund officer who decides whether a payment should be made. The officer can use his or her discretion in each case. The discretionary payments are also **cash-limited**. This means that each office is allocated a certain amount of money each year and cannot spend any more. The Social Fund officer must decide each case bearing this in mind.

Non-discretionary payments

Funeral payments

Funeral payments can be claimed by people who are getting Income Support, Housing Benefit or Family Credit. The payment is for the full basic cost of a funeral. In deciding how much to pay, the Department of Social Security will take account of any money available to pay for a funeral. This includes any insurance policies and money from the dead person's estate. Savings over £500 (April 1992) belonging to the person responsible for the funeral are also taken into account. For people over 60 the amount is £1000.

Maternity expenses

Maternity expenses can be claimed by people on Family Credit or Income Support who are expecting a baby or who have just had a baby. The payment is £100 (April 1992). If the claimant has savings over £500, the payment is reduced by £1 for every pound of capital over £500.

Cold Weather Payment

The **Cold Weather Payment** is paid in a period of exceptionally cold weather. This means that the average temperature for each day is at or below 0 degrees Celsius for a period of seven days running. People who qualify are those on Income Support and receiving one of the following premiums: pensioner premium, disability premium, higher pensioner premium, severe disability premium and disabled child premium. People with children under five also qualify. The payment (April 1992) is £6 for each week of cold weather. The amount is reduced if people have savings over £500, or over £1000 in the case of people over 60.

Discretionary payments

Community Care Grants

Community Care Grants do not have to be repaid. But the Community Care Grant is a discretionary and cash-limited payment. The Social Fund officer will therefore make a decision based on the needs of the people applying and the amount of money remaining in the fund. Payments can be made in a number of circumstances. People who are moving out of residential care, for example a mental-handicap hospital, can receive help with costs such as fuel connections or essential items like a cooker. Payments can be made to help people stay in the community, for example to meet the costs of minor repairs or to buy essential furniture. Grants can also be made to help with exceptional pressures on families caused by disability, chronic sickness or major family changes. In urgent situations, travel expenses can be met, for example to go to a funeral or to visit a sick relative.

Budgeting Loans

Budgeting Loans are paid to people who have been on Income Support for at least 26 weeks. They are again discretionary and cash-limited. Since the payment is a loan, the Social Fund officer will include assessment of the person's ability to pay in the decision as to whether or not to give a loan. The loan will be repaid by deductions from benefit. No interest is charged on the loan. Budgeting Loans are for large items which cannot be paid for out of weekly benefit, such as a new cooker or a bed. The loan can be between £30 and £1000 (April 1992).

Crisis Loans

Crisis Loans can be given to anyone, not only those on benefits. They are for emergency needs, for example following a flood or a fire. They are given where money is needed to prevent risk to health and safety.

4.4 Housing Benefit

Housing Benefit is paid to people on a low income who rent their home. It can be claimed by people in full-time work, as well as by those people living on Income Support or other benefits. It is paid by the local authority housing department. Housing Benefit cannot be claimed by people with savings over £16 000. People with savings over £3000 but less than £16 000 (April 1992) will have the amount of Housing Benefit they claim reduced. Every £250 will count as income of £1 a week.

Calculating Housing Benefit involves a number of steps.

Step 1: the rent

The first step is to assess the amount of *rent* which can be claimed. The maximum is 100 per cent of the rent.

There are rules about what counts as rent. For example, fuel charges or water rates cannot be included. In some cases the council can restrict the benefit because the rent is unreasonably high. Deductions are made where non-dependants share the house.

There are a number of situations in which people can claim Housing Benefit

Step 2: money coming in

The second step is to look at *capital and income*. As described above, £1 of income a week is assumed for each £250 of savings between £3000 and £16 000. Income is counted after deductions for tax and national insurance.

Some income is ignored:

- Attendance Allowance;
- Mobility Allowance;
- Social Fund payments;
- actual income from savings;
- of earnings, £5 for a single person, £10 for a couple, £15 for a person with a disability (April 1992 rates);
- £4 income from a sub-tenant.

Step 3: applicable amounts

The third step is to consider the *applicable amount* for the person or family. This is calculated in the same way as for Income Support, with personal allowances and premiums (see section 4.1).

If the claimant's income is the same as or below the total applicable amount, the rent will be paid in full. This would be the case for someone on Income Support. For people with a higher income, a reduction is made. The amount paid is reduced by 65 per cent of the difference between the income and the applicable amount. In other words, the maximum Housing Benefit is reduced by 65 pence for every £1 over the applicable amount.

EXAMPLE 1

Martin is single and unemployed. He is 26 and receives £42.45 in Income Support. He lives alone and pays a rent of £40 a week.

The applicable amount for him is £42.45 a week. This is the same as his income, so he gets all his rent paid in Housing Benefit.

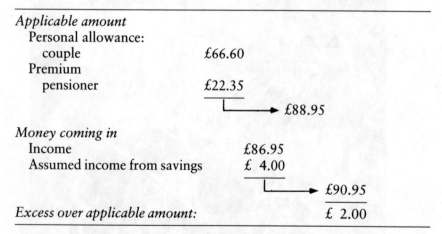

Applicable amount		
Personal allowance:		
couple	£66.60	
Premium		
pensioner	£22.35	
		£88.95
Money coming in		
Income	£86.95	
Assumed income from savings	£ 4.00	
		£90.95
Excess over applicable amount:		£ 2.00

The money coming in is *higher* than the applicable amount, so the Housing Benefit is reduced by 65 pence for each £1 above the applicable amount. In this case, this is £1.30.

Full rent	£50.00
Reduction	£ 1.30
Housing benefit paid:	£48.70

WORDCHECK

Social Fund A fund which can provide loans and grants for buying larger items or in times of crisis.

discretionary benefit A benefit awarded to some and not to others, the decision being taken by an official according to the merits of the individual case.

cash-limited Dependent on the money available, as in the case of some parts of the Social Fund – a certain sum of money is available initially; once this has been spent, no more payments can be made.

applicable amount The amount of money a household is calculated to need: the income is assessed and compared with this to decide how much benefit is to be paid.

premium A part of Income Support, for people with extra needs such as older people or one-parent families.

personal allowance The other part of Income Support, calculated on the basis of age.

EXAMPLE 2

Mr and Mrs Wong are aged 62 and 65. They have an income of £86.95 a week from a pension. They live in a council flat and pay £50.00 a week in rent. They have savings of £4000.

4.5 Benefits for families in work

Child Benefit and One-Parent Benefit

All parents are entitled to **Child Benefit**. This is paid for each child, with a higher amount for the first child. Lone parents can also claim **One-Parent Benefit**, which is £5.85 (April 1992). This is the same whatever the number of children. Child Benefit lasts until the child is sixteen, or nineteen if in full-time education.

Family Credit

People with dependent children can claim **Family Credit** if they are on a low wage. For Family Credit, people must be in full-time work, which is classed as 16 hours a week or more. Family Credit is not paid to people who have more than £8000 in savings. It is reduced for people with between £3000 and £8000. The maximum Family Credit is made up of an adult credit and credits for children, depending on age. The adult credit is the same whether there are two parents or one.

The applicable amount is set by the government each year. People whose income is *on or below* the applicable amount will receive the maximum Family Credit for their size and age of family. People whose income is *over* the applicable amount have the maximum Family Credit reduced by 70 per cent of the difference. In other words, the maximum is reduced by 70 pence for every £1 someone earns over the applicable amount, £66.60 (April 1992). The income considered is the net wages; Child Benefit is not counted. Where someone has savings of between £3000 and £8000, £1 of income per week is assumed for each £250.

Family Credit is a **passport benefit**, giving automatic entitlement to some other benefits. These are free prescriptions, free dental care, free sight tests and vouchers for glasses. For this reason it may be worth claiming Family Credit even if the weekly payments will be low. Family Credit is paid for 26 weeks, regardless of any changes in circumstances. If someone is thinking of claiming in March it might be worthwhile waiting until April, when the rates are adjusted. Similarly it is best to claim when income is at its lowest.

Housing Benefit; Social Fund

Families on a low income may also be eligible for **Housing Benefit** and help from the **Social Fund** (see sections 4.3 and 4.4).

WORDCHECK

applicable amount The amount of money a household is calculated to need: the income is assessed and compared with this to decide how much benefit is to be paid.
Social Fund A fund which can provide loans and grants for buying larger items or in times of crisis.
passport benefit A social security benefit which gives automatic entitlement to another benefit.

One-Parent Benefit is not means-tested so the claim form is fairly short

Claim One Parent Benefit on this form

FORM CH11A

Please read these notes before you fill in the form.
Do not claim for a baby before the birth.

You can only get One Parent Benefit if you get Child Benefit as well. If you have not yet claimed Child Benefit get a claim form CH2 from your local Social Security office and send it in with this form.

If you want any help filling in this form please get in touch with your Social Security office.

Please write as clearly as possible, using CAPITALS.

1 About you

Your Child Benefit number if you know it

Numbers	Letters

► If you are already getting Child Benefit at a Post Office the number is on the front of your Child Benefit book

► If you are already getting Child Benefit paid into a bank or building society the number is at the top of the letter we sent you about this

Your full name and address

A Your title – for example Mrs

B Your surname

C Your other names

D is the name in question **B** the same as any of these **3**

1 the name on the front of your Child Benefit book?

or **2** the name on the letter we sent you about getting your Child Benefit paid into a bank or building society?

or **3** the name on the claim form for Child Benefit that we sent you?

Please write **Yes** or **No** here

E Your address including Postcode

01

F Is your address in question **E** the same as any of these **3**

1 the address on your Child Benefit book?

or **2** the address on the letter we sent you about getting your money paid into a bank or building society?

or **3** the address on the claim form for Child Benefit that we sent you?

Please write **Yes** or **No** here

G Your telephone number and STD code if you know it.

EXAMPLE 1

Mr and Mrs Ram have three children, aged 5, 7 and 13. Mrs Ram does not work and Mr Ram has a net income of £100 a week. The family has no savings. The maximum credit for the family is:

Adult credit	£41.00
Child aged 5	£10.40
Child aged 7	£10.40
Child aged 13	£17.25
	£79.05

Mr Ram's wages are more than the applicable amount of £66.60. The excess is £33.40 (£100.00 − £66.60). 70 per cent of this difference (that is, 70 per cent of £33.40) is £23.38. The maximum Family Credit is therefore reduced by £23.38. The Family Credit payable is *£55.67* (£79.05 − £23.38).

The family's total income will be made up of the wages, the Family Credit and the Child Benefit. They will also be entitled to free prescriptions, dental care, sight tests and glasses.

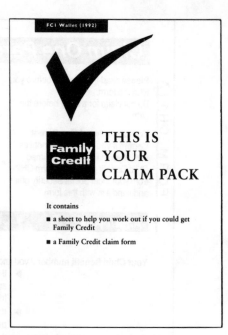

FCi Wallet (1992)

Family Credit

THIS IS YOUR CLAIM PACK

It contains

■ a sheet to help you work out if you could get Family Credit

■ a Family Credit claim form

Family Credit is paid to working families with low incomes

See if you might qualify

Please look at the second page of your Child Benefit order book. It will tell you if you may be able to get Family Credit.

or If you are paid your Child Benefit directly into an account, look at the letter we sent you about this. It will tell you if you may be able to get Family Credit.

or Pick out your family in the chart opposite. Claim if the amount of money coming into your home each week is the amount shown or less.

- These amounts apply to both lone parents and couples
- The chart is just a guide – even if your family is not shown here, you could still qualify
- If you're still in doubt, fill in the claim form.

Money coming in includes

- Take-home pay
- Business profits
  after allowable expenses
- Social Security benefits
  but not Child Benefit
  or One Parent Benefit
  or Attendance Allowance
  or Disability Living Allowance
  or Housing Benefit
  or Community Charge Benefit
- Other money
  for example, maintenance (except the first £15) or money from boarders or sub-tenants

KEY

Child under 11 years

Child between 11-15 years

Child between 16-17 years at school

Child 18 years at school

£139 or less	£154 or less	£169 or less	£193 or less
£149 or less	£163 or less	£178 or less	£203 or less
£155 or less	£169 or less	£184 or less	£219 or less
£167 or less	£173 or less	£188 or less	£221 or less
	£179 or less	£194 or less	£237 or less
	£191 or less	£222 or less	
	£197 or less		

DSS guidance on who is entitled to Family Credit

4.6 Benefits for people out of work

There are two main benefits for people who are out of work: Unemployment Benefit and Income Support.

Unemployment Benefit

Unemployment Benefit can be claimed by people who are out of work and who have paid enough national insurance contributions. The main rule is that national insurance contributions must have been paid for two years before claiming Unemployment Benefit. In one of these two years, the contributions may have been credited rather than actually paid. This might happen for instance where a person is caring for someone who is disabled and receiving Invalid Care Allowance, or where someone is on certain training courses.

To qualify for Unemployment Benefit, people must be available for work and 'actively seeking work'. This means that people must 'take steps' to find work, such as looking in newspapers and applying for jobs. Someone who is thought not to be trying hard enough will be sent a warning and asked to attend a review.

People who give up a job by choice, or who lose a job through misconduct, can lose benefit for up to 26 weeks. People who turn down offers of work without an acceptable reason can be disqualified from receiving benefit. Low pay is not considered an acceptable reason for turning down a job.

Unemployment Benefit is not paid for the first three days of unemployment. It is paid for one year only.

Income Support

After Unemployment Benefit has run out, **Income Support** can be claimed. People who are not entitled to Unemployment Benefit – because they have not paid contributions, for example – can claim Income Support.

People may also claim Income Support *in addition to* Unemployment Benefit. If the Unemployment Benefit does not bring a family up to the level set by Income Support, then this benefit will be paid as well (see section 4.1).

Housing Benefit and the Social Fund

People who are unemployed and renting their home will be eligible for **Housing Benefit** to help with the rent (see section 4.4). They may also be able to get help from the **Social Fund** (see section 4.3).

TO DO

Consider whether the following people would be eligible for Unemployment Benefit. If not, is there another benefit they could claim instead?

(a) Harry has worked for fifteen years, but has just been made redundant.

(b) Suki Adenwalla left college at 21 after having been in full-time education since finishing school.

(c) Janice gave up a full-time job she had had for five years in order to care for an elderly aunt. A year later, the aunt has died.

4.7 Benefits for people who are sick or disabled

Statutory sick pay

When someone with a job is ill, the employer must pay sick pay. This is known as **statutory sick pay** (SSP). There are two rates of SSP: a higher rate for people who earn more than £190 a week gross, and a lower rate for people who earn between £54 and £189.99 a week (April 1992 rates). People who earn less than £54 do not pay national insurance contributions and are not eligible for SSP. Statutory sick pay is not paid for the first three days and lasts for 28 weeks.

Many employers are more generous than the law requires them to be and have their own occupational sick pay schemes. These often pay full wages for a limited period of time and then half wages for another period.

Sickness Benefit, Invalidity Benefit and Invalidity Pension

Most people are eligible for statutory sick pay. Those who are not, but who have paid enough national insurance contributions, can claim **Sickness Benefit** from the Department of Social Security.

After entitlement to statutory sick pay or Sickness Benefit ends, someone who is still incapable of work can move on to **Invalidity Benefit**. There are two parts to this. The first is the **Invalidity Pension**. In addition, people below a certain age – under 60 in the case of men and under 55 in the case of women – get an Invalidity Allowance on top of the Invalidity Pension. The amount depends on the age at which the illness or disability started. These payments continue as long as the person is unable to work, until the ages of 65 for a woman and 70 for a man.

Severe Disablement Allowance

The **Severe Disablement Allowance** is paid to people who cannot claim Invalidity Benefit because they haven't paid enough national insurance contributions. It is paid after someone has been incapable of work for 28 weeks. There is a basic payment and an age-related addition.

Disability Living Allowance (DLA)

The **Disability Living Allowance** is a benefit introduced in 1992, replacing the Attendance Allowance and the Mobility Allowance. It has two parts: a care component and a mobility component.

The care component

The care component is paid to people who are disabled and need attention from a carer. To qualify, people must need help with basic things such as washing and eating, or need supervision to avoid danger. There is a lower age limit of 2 and an upper age limit of 65. (Older people who need help can claim the Attendance Allowance, which has two rates – a higher rate for those who need help by day *and* night, and a lower rate for those who need help in the day *or* the night.) To get the Disability Living Allowance, people must have been needing help for 3 months and be likely to need it for another 6 months. This qualifying period is waived in the case of people with terminal illnesses.

The care component is paid at three rates. The top rate is paid to people who need attendance by day and night. The middle rate is for those who need help by day *or* night. The lowest rate can be claimed by someone under 65 who needs help for part of the day or who cannot manage to cook a meal. The cooking test does not apply to a child under 16: a child will qualify if he or she needs more attention than other children of the same age.

No medical examination is needed to qualify for these benefits, and the payments are not affected by savings or other income.

The mobility component

The mobility component of the DLA is for people who have trouble getting about or who need to be accompanied outside. This includes people who cannot walk, those who are deaf and blind, and people with severe learning difficulties.

Claimants must be over 5. You cannot make a fresh claim if over the age of 65, but people who have been receiving the benefit from a younger age will continue to get it.

There are two rates for this part of the DLA: a higher and a lower rate, paid according to the extent to which a person's ability to get about is limited.

The higher rate of the mobility component of the DLA can be used to lease or buy a car from a charitable organisation called **Motability**. Under this scheme the benefit is paid direct to the charity.

The Disability Working Allowance (DWA)

The **Disability Working Allowance** is for people aged over 16 who work at least 16 hours a week. People must be 'disadvantaged' by their disability in getting a job. This includes physical and mental disabilities. The benefit is means-tested on the basis of savings and income. The same rules and levels of income apply as for other means-tested benefits, and the amount is calculated in a similar way to Family Credit. It is however paid to all people with disabilities, whether or not they have children. Like Family Credit, the benefit is paid for 26 weeks, regardless of any changes in circumstances. To qualify for the benefit the person must have been getting a disability benefit in the 8 weeks before claiming DWA.

Disablement Benefit

There are different benefits for people who are injured at work or who have one of the designated industrial diseases. **Disablement Benefit** can be claimed by people 90 days after an industrial injury or the start of an industrial disease.

The amount paid depends on the degree of the disability. This is assessed in terms of percentages. As an indication, the loss of both hands is classed as 100 per cent, whereas the loss of a thumb counts as 30 per cent disablement.

Constant Attendance Allowance

There is also a **Constant Attendance Allowance**, which can be claimed on top of a 100 per cent Disablement Benefit by someone who needs constant attendance. There is a higher rate and a lower rate. The rate given depends on the degree of disability and the level of attendance required.

Income Support, Housing Benefit and the Social Fund

People with disabilities may receive **Income Support** (section 4.1), **Housing Benefit** (section 4.4) and help from the **Social Fund** (section 4.3). Income Support includes disability premiums which can be claimed by people receiving the Attendance Allowance.

Finding out more: benefits for the disabled

★   For further information on the Motability scheme, contact the organisation directly.

★   People with disabilities wanting information on benefits (and anything else concerned with disability) can contact DIAL (Disablement Information and Advice Lines). The local address should be in the telephone book; the national address is given in the appendix.

★   For information on benefits for people with disabilities, see the *Disability Rights Handbook*. This is available from the Disability Alliance.

4.8 Help for people with disabilities

The Independent Living Fund

The **Independent Living Fund** was set up to help severely disabled people to live in the community. It can provide assistance for people who wish to leave a residential home or those who want to stay in their own homes. People must be over 16 to claim, and be receiving the higher level of the Attendance Allowance. They must be on a low income and have no one at home who is able to care for them. When an application is made, a worker from the Independent Living Fund will visit and make an assessment.

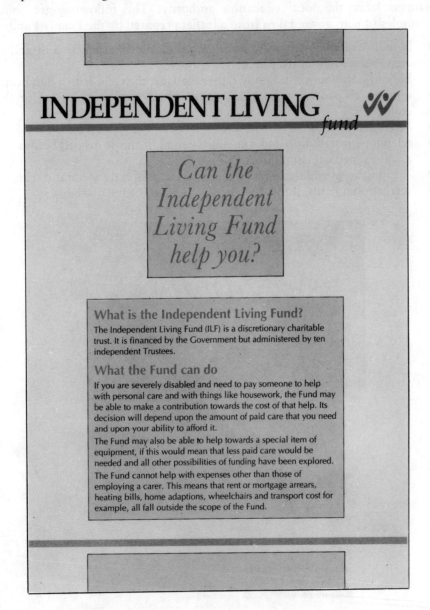

INDEPENDENT LIVING *fund*

Can the Independent Living Fund help you?

What is the Independent Living Fund?

The Independent Living Fund (ILF) is a discretionary charitable trust. It is financed by the Government but administered by ten independent Trustees.

What the Fund can do

If you are severely disabled and need to pay someone to help with personal care and with things like housework, the Fund may be able to make a contribution towards the cost of that help. Its decision will depend upon the amount of paid care that you need and upon your ability to afford it.

The Fund may also be able to help towards a special item of equipment, if this would mean that less paid care would be needed and all other possibilities of funding have been explored.

The Fund cannot help with expenses other than those of employing a carer. This means that rent or mortgage arrears, heating bills, home adaptions, wheelchairs and transport cost for example, all fall outside the scope of the Fund.

The Independent Living Fund leaflet

4.9 Help for families with a disabled child

The Family Fund

The **Family Fund** is financed by the government but run by an independent trust, the Joseph Rowntree Foundation in York. Payments are made to families which include a severely disabled child. The trust employs social workers who visit families to advise and to assess their needs.

Families are helped with things they would not otherwise be able to afford. The Fund does not provide for anything which could be obtained from another source, such as payments to do with education which could be claimed from the local education authority. The following are some examples of help given, taken from a leaflet prepared by the Family Fund:

* laundry equipment, for example a washing machine where a disability creates a lot of extra washing;
* holidays, for the whole family rather than just the child with a handicap;
* outings, to provide relaxation for the family and stimulation for the child;
* driving lessons, for a parent;
* telephone installation and sometimes rental, if this is needed because of a child's medical condition;
* clothing and bedding, where a handicap creates extra wear and tear;
* recreational items, if these are needed because of the disability.

family fund

The Family Fund

The Family Fund is a government fund

independently run by the Joseph

Rowntree Foundation to help families

who are caring for a child who is very

severely handicapped by a disability

The Family Fund helps families with a child with a severe handicap

4.10 Benefits for carers

Invalid Care Allowance

The **Invalid Care Allowance** is paid to people caring for someone who receives the Attendance Allowance. The carer need not be living with the person, but must be caring for him or her for 35 hours a week or more. The carer must be between the ages of 16 and 65, and not in work or full-time education.

4.11 Benefits for older people

Retirement pension

The rules about retirement pensions are quite complicated so just a basic outline will be given here.

To get a retirement pension there are two basic rules. First, people must be over retirement age, which is 60 for a woman and 65 for a man. They must also meet the national insurance requirements. This means people must have paid national insurance contributions for most of their working life. In certain circumstances, national insurance contributions are credited – for example when someone stays at home to care for children.

People may also be entitled to additional payments. There is an additional pension, paid under the **State Earnings-Related Pension Scheme** (**SERPS**). This is based on contributions since 1978 and the amount paid depends on the wages earned. Some people do not pay into this scheme – they are **contracted out** – because they have a different pension scheme, often through their work. These people receive the basic state pension plus an occupational or individual pension. An earlier scheme was the **graduated pension** scheme and some people receive extra money as a result of having paid into this when they were working between 1961 and 1975.

People over 80 have the princely sum of 25 pence a week added to their basic pension. People over 80 also qualify for a pension, even if they have not paid any contributions to national insurance.

Older people can continue working and still receive their retirement pension, but their pension will be taxed. They can, however, opt out of national insurance payments. It is also possible to defer pension payments for up to five years after retirement age and earn extra pension instead. The increase is about 7.5 per cent a year.

Income Support, Housing Benefit and the Social Fund

Older people also qualify for **Income Support** if their income falls below the level set for someone in their circumstances. There are premiums for older people, depending on age (see section 4.1). People may also qualify for Housing Benefit (section 4.4) if they rent a house or flat, and for help from the Social Fund (section 4.3).

Some older people will qualify for benefits awarded to people with disabilities (section 4.8).

Finding out more: benefits for older people

★   Age Concern produces free leaflets on benefits and pensions for older people.

★   Age Concern also produces an excellent book on benefits and other sources of finance for older people. This is called *Your Rights*. It is updated each year and is on sale in bookshops. It can also be bought directly from Age Concern.

4.12 Help with the cost of residential care

People who need to live in a residential or nursing home and who are on a low income can claim financial help from the Department of Social Security.

There are two types of residential care (see Chapter 2). In a **local authority home** there is a sliding scale of charges based on how much the person can afford to pay. There is a minimum charge, and an elderly person on the basic pension with savings of less than £1250 (April 1992) would have to pay this minimum. If someone had less than this, they would receive Income Support which would bring them up to the basic level and allow them some spending money to keep each week. The system is the same if the local authority pays for someone to go into a private home or one run by a voluntary organisation.

The Department of Social Security will also pay fees in a **private residential or nursing home**. The claimant must have a low income and savings of less than £8000. The fees payable depend on the type of care needed. People will also receive a small weekly sum to cover personal expenses.

4.13 Benefits for widows

A woman whose husband has died qualifies for widows' benefits if he paid national insurance contributions.

Widows' Payment

For a **Widows' Payment** the husband must have paid national insurance for one year. The woman must be under 60 or else the husband must not have been eligible for a retirement pension at the time of his death. The payment is a one-off lump-sum.

Widowed Mothers' Allowance

The **Widowed Mothers' Allowance** is a weekly benefit paid to widows who are pregnant or who have children eligible for Child Benefit. The husband must have paid national insurance contributions for most of his working life.

Widows' Pension

A **Widows' Pension** is paid to widows aged at least 45 at the time of their husband's death or at the time the Widowed Mothers' Allowance stops. Additions based on earnings after 1979 may be payable.

4.14 Benefits for women expecting a baby

Statutory maternity pay

Women in paid employment who become pregnant are entitled to **statutory maternity pay (SMP)**. This is paid to all women who have worked with the same employer for at least 26 weeks and who are expecting a child in 11 weeks' time or who have recently had a baby. The higher rate of SMP is paid for the first 6 weeks – this is nine-tenths of the woman's average weekly wage. Then a lower rate is paid for 7 weeks (although there are detailed rules about when the benefit can be claimed). Some employers have a more generous scheme for maternity pay, with longer periods and higher payments.

Maternity Allowance

Women who have recently given up their job or changed jobs can claim **Maternity Allowance**.

Maternity Grant

Women on Income Support or Family Credit can claim a **Maternity Grant** of £100 (April 1992) from the Social Fund.

TO DO

Consider those of your clients who are in receipt of welfare benefits.

- Which benefits do they receive?
- Looking at the information in this chapter, which benefits are they entitled to?
- If there is a difference, what are the reasons for this? Could you, and if so should you, do anything about this difference?

TO DO

What benefits, if any, would the people in the following situations be entitled to?

(a) Judrani, a 16-year-old boy who has left school this month and is living with his family.

(b) Maggie, a single parent, not working, who is caring for two children at home.

(c) Mr Shang, a man who has just been made redundant after working for ten years.

(d) Kika, a woman who started work three months ago and has lost her job. Her husband earns £200 a week.

(e) Lindsay, a woman who gave up work to care for her elderly and disabled mother.

(f) The Wells family – the father works in a well-paid job and the mother has a part-time job. One of the three children is severely disabled and confined to a wheelchair.

(g) Robyn, a woman with three children under sixteen, whose husband has died.

(h) Peter, a man of 68 who has had a lifelong disability and has never worked.

(i) Jill, a woman who changed jobs, then found she was pregnant.

(j) Mike, a man with a mental handicap who is moving from a hospital into the community.

4.15   Educational grants

There are two types of grants for education: major and minor awards. Local authorities set their own rules for minor awards and the payments are discretionary. **Minor awards** are for courses which are non-advanced – this is anything below degree level and includes A-levels and Access courses. These grants are means-tested and may be just to cover the fees or may include living expenses. **Major awards** are for full-time degree and degree-equivalent courses at polytechnics and universities. These grants are not discretionary and people are entitled to them when they are accepted on to the qualifying courses.

Grants for full-time advanced courses are means-tested. For young people, an assessment will be made of the parents' income. This takes account of the number of people dependent on the income, and of some other costs such as mortgage interest payments. Parents' income is not looked at if the student is 'independent': there are several criteria for this. One is that the student must be aged over 25. Younger people are seen as being independent if they have supported themselves by a job for three years or for two or more periods adding up to three years. Others are seen as independent if they have been married for two years, or have been in care with the local authority for two years. The grant pays for fees and living costs.

Students in higher education can also apply for **interest-free loans**, to be paid back after they have finished studying.

Colleges and universities may have funds which can help poorer students with fees. The Open University, for example, has such a scheme. The local education authority may also help with the costs of study with the Open University.

WORDCHECK

minor award   A grant for a non-advanced course of education, including A-levels; this award is discretionary and local education authorities vary in their policies.

major award   A grant for an advanced course of education: local authorities *must* give these to people who have places on degree-level courses.

means-tested benefit   A benefit awarded to some and not to others, according to the individual client's income and savings.

discretionary benefit   A benefit awarded to some and not to others, the decision being taken by an official according to the merits of the individual case.

TO FIND OUT

1   Contact the local education authority to find out the policy on paying fees and expenses for people studying at colleges of further education, but taking courses below degree level.

2   Contact the local college and find out what help they can offer to people on low incomes.

5 Daily living

Our world is becoming increasingly competitive and fast-moving. People are expected to be able to look after themselves and to get ahead. It seems that people have less time for, and show less patience towards, those whose disability or learning difficulty means they cannot move at the world's pace. At the same time, there is a move away from the idea that such people should live apart from society, in residential institutions. The current thinking is that, as far as possible, people with disabilities or learning difficulties should live at home in the local community.

This chapter is about the services and facilities which aim to enable people with disabilities and other special needs to live full and independent lives. If you are involved in providing care you need to know something of the range of services available. Your task as a care worker is to co-ordinate services into a complete **package of care** which meets the needs of the individual person. This will involve private and voluntary organisations as well as services provided within the social services department or by the health authority. Other people, such as community psychiatric nurses, will also have this sort of role.

Relevant legislation

There are two important laws affecting people with disabilities. The first is the 1970 Chronically Sick and Disabled Persons Act 1970. This requires social services departments to assess the needs of people with disabilities living in their area. The sorts of needs to be considered are practical needs, for personal care, and for help with domestic tasks and meals; transport needs; and leisure and communication needs, such as provision of a television and a telephone.

The second, and more recent, Act is the 1986 Disabled Persons (Services, Consultation and Representation) Act. Unfortunately for people with disabilities the government has delayed parts of this Act from coming into force. The Act gives certain rights to people with disabilities. Some of the main rights already in force are as follows:

- When assessing a disabled person's need for services, the local authority has a duty to take account of a carer's ability to provide care.
- The local authority has a duty to give information to people with disabilities. This includes information on the services provided within the social services department, those provided by other government departments, and those offered by voluntary and private organisations.
- When people are brought on to council committees to represent people with disabilities, there must be consultation with organisations of people with disabilities.

5.1 Getting about

Access officers check that new buildings meet the requirements for people with disabilities

Access

The 1970 Chronically Sick and Disabled Persons Act made it a duty for designers and owners of new buildings to consider the needs of people with disabilities. A further development came in 1981. The Disabled Persons Act of that year gave planning authorities the duty of drawing people's attention to provisions relating to access. This must be done when planning permission is granted.

These provisions were extended in 1985. Certain new buildings must now provide access and facilities for people with disabilities. These include offices, shops, single-storey factories, educational buildings and others which admit the public. Local authorities have begun to employ **access officers** to oversee these regulations.

Finding out more: access for disabled people

★ For further information on the legislation and regulations concerning access to buildings, contact the Disabled Living Foundation.
★ There are local guides to a number of towns and cities, written for people with disabilities. These are produced locally, but under the umbrella of the Royal Association for Disability and Rehabilitation (RADAR). These guides give details of public buildings, including information on door widths, the number of steps in the building, and the toilet facilities. A list of the booklets available can be obtained from RADAR.

Mobility aids

Walking aids such as walking sticks, crutches and Zimmer frames can be borrowed from the health authority or from voluntary organisations such as the Red Cross. Wheelchairs are also available for loan. *Motability* provides a hire-purchase scheme for people receiving the Mobility Allowance to enable them to buy electric wheelchairs.

TO DO

1 Survey your local area to see how accessible it is for people confined to wheelchairs. Check widths of doorways, numbers of steps, availability of lifts, and access to toilets.

2 If possible, borrow a wheelchair and work with a colleague, finding out what it is like to negotiate a town or village with a wheelchair. Set yourself a number of tasks, such as buying a stamp, using a phone, going to the toilet, having a drink, or getting a bus.

As an alternative, you could try the same tasks with a pram. Using a pram will not give you the same insight into the psychological difficulties of being in a wheelchair, but some of the practical problems are similar.

3 Find out whether there is a guide written for people with disabilities trying to use facilities in your area. If not, you could consider writing one. Local schools, colleges or voluntary organisations may be prepared to help. Local businesses might help with the costs of printing and distribution.

TO DO

1 Make a survey of local travel facilities. Include the following:

- bus services;
- taxis;
- coaches;
- trains;
- the underground (if applicable);
- social services transport;
- transport by Dial-a-Ride or other voluntary organisations.

Find out what facilities are available and what concessionary fares there are.

2 Talk to clients with disabilities. What services do they use? How well are these services tailored to their needs? How could the services be improved?

Special services

Dial-a-Ride is a door-to-door transport system for people with disabilities who are unable to use public transport. Bookings are made in advance, by telephone. A number of voluntary organisations offer the service of volunteer drivers using their own cars. In some cases these are free, in others a small charge is made. The WRVS provides a shopping service with specially adapted minibuses. In some cases the health authority and the social services provide transport. Again, there may be a charge.

Finding out more: special services

There are three organisations which can give information on Dial-a-Ride and other similar schemes. These are:

- Community Transport Association;
- The National Advisory Unit;
- London Dial-a-Ride Users Association.

5.2 Leisure

There are a number of services and organisations working to help people with disabilities to participate in leisure activities.

Books, radios and televisions

Most local authorities provide a **travelling library** service which brings library books to people's homes. Social services may be able to provide radios and televisions for people with disabilities. An organisation called *British Wireless for the Blind* will lend radios free of charge to blind people. For those who are housebound, there is *Wireless for the Bedridden*, which loans radios and televisions.

Sports

Many sports centres have facilities for people with disabilities. The RADAR guides to local areas (referred to above, under 'Access') provide information on the accessibility of sports facilities as well as other services. There are also many specialist organisations offering information and special provision for people with disabilities. Some examples are listed below. The Disabled Living Foundation can provide up-to-date information on services available. The foundation has leaflets and a comprehensive *Information Service Handbook*.

Holidays

Various organisations can provide information on holidays for disabled people and their carers. It may be possible to get financial help towards a holiday from social services or from a charitable organisation. Organisations for specific illnesses and conditions, such as the Kidney Patients Association, may have special arrangements to help people with holidays.

PHAB (Physically Handicapped and Able-Bodied) is an organisation which tries to break down barriers and stereotypes by bringing people with disabilities and able-bodied people together. The organisation consists of local groups which arrange social clubs, outings and holidays.

Finding out more: holidays

★ Age Concern produces a factsheet on *Holidays for Older People*.
★ The Holiday Care Service is an information service on holiday and transport facilities for people with disabilities. It also gives information on financial help.
★ There are two useful books available from W. H. Smith or RADAR. They are: *Holidays in the British Isles: a guide for disabled people* and *Holidays and Travel Abroad: a guide for disabled people*. New editions of both are published each year.
★ The *MENCAP Holiday Guide* is available from the MENCAP Holiday Office.

TO DO

One of the problems for people with disabilities in using leisure facilities is that of access. Survey the recreational facilities in your area from the point of view of a person in a wheelchair. Look at:

- cinemas;
- bingo halls;
- theatres;
- discos;
- nightclubs;
- sports centres;
- swimming pools;
- pubs.

5.3 Care and support

The majority of people who are older or who have a disability live in their own homes. They may need help with domestic or personal tasks. This section looks at the services available to help. The section also looks at facilities providing care, on a non-residential basis, in day centres; and at an innovatory system of care in another person's home.

Social services

Social workers are often the starting point for these kinds of services. They assess the needs of the individual or household. They provide counselling and advice on welfare rights and other services. They also co-ordinate services and recommend and refer people to other parts of social services or the health service.

Help at home

One of the most valuable services run by the social services department is the **home-help service**. Home helps provide help with domestic tasks such as cleaning, washing and shopping. They may also carry out some personal tasks. In some areas the home-help service is free, but in other areas charges have been introduced.

Many areas are also now developing home-care services. These work on similar principles to the home-help service. The worker visits the client in his or her own home. Home-care workers are however more involved with personal care, such as dressing and bathing, than are traditional home helps. Home-care services allow someone to remain in the community who might otherwise have had to go into a residential home.

In addition to home helps provided by the local authority, there are also private organisations offering a similar service. One example is Independent Home Care Services, in Essex. There is an hourly charge for this service. Voluntary organisations also work in this field. In some areas, Age Concern runs a service providing home care.

Relief for carers

Crossroads Care Attendance Scheme is a national voluntary organisation funded jointly by health authorities and social services. It provides relief for carers of people with disabilities by helping with practical tasks. Care attendants are trained and employed to take over the role of the carer and to give a break when this is most needed.

Meals

The **meals-on-wheels** service delivers hot meals at midday to older people and others living in the community. The service is usually administered by the social services department but run by a voluntary organisation such as the WRVS. There is a charge for the meals, but this is usually less than the cost. Referrals are through doctors and social workers. Social services assess clients to see whether they qualify for the service.

Incontinence

For people who have problems with incontinence, there are laundry schemes. These may be attached to the home-help service or run by the health authority. Laundry is collected and delivered. The health authority may also supply various items such as commodes and incontinence pads. Some areas employ a **continence nurse advisor** to provide counselling, advice and information.

Day care

There are various types of **day centres**, provided by social services, the health authority and voluntary organisations. Older people may attend day centres attached to residential homes. These would allow a carer to work in the day or simply to have a break. Organisations such as Age Concern run centres providing recreational activities and usually a midday meal. There are also day centres which concentrate on teaching living skills to help people with disabilities or those with learning difficulties.

Some areas have innovative schemes, such as *Homeshare Daycare* which runs in Ipswich. This provides day care for elderly people in family homes.

Some areas have innovative schemes for day care

TO THINK ABOUT

There have been various suggestions about different ways of providing and delivering services. One suggestion is that people could be given money and could themselves employ the help they need, instead of being given services by the local authority.

Is this a good idea? What would be the advantages and disadvantages of this form of service delivery? What are the views of your colleagues and your clients?

The scheme employs experienced people who take each a small number of elderly people into their homes on a daily basis. Transport is provided. This scheme works as an alternative to day care in residential homes and day centres.

A different scheme for children with learning difficulties is **shared care**. Here carers are recruited to care for children for up to 20 days a year. This gives the parents a break, as well as providing wider experiences for the child.

Finding out more: help at home

★ Age Concern produces a useful factsheet called *Finding Help at Home*. It is available from the Information and Policy Department of Age Concern England.

5.4 Equipment to help with daily living

Occupational therapists are employed by social services and by health authorities. Their work is concerned with helping people with disabilities to live as independently as possible. They visit people at home to assess their situation and needs. They can teach people alternative approaches to tasks and problems. They also advise people on special equipment which will make things easier.

There is a vast range of special equipment designed for people with disabilities. Aids exist for most personal and domestic tasks. Some examples are mechanical chairs to help people stand from sitting; special cutlery and plates for those who have problems with hand movements; and equipment to make bathing or showering safer and easier. Aids can be borrowed from the local authority or bought.

There is a vast range of special equipment for people with disabilities

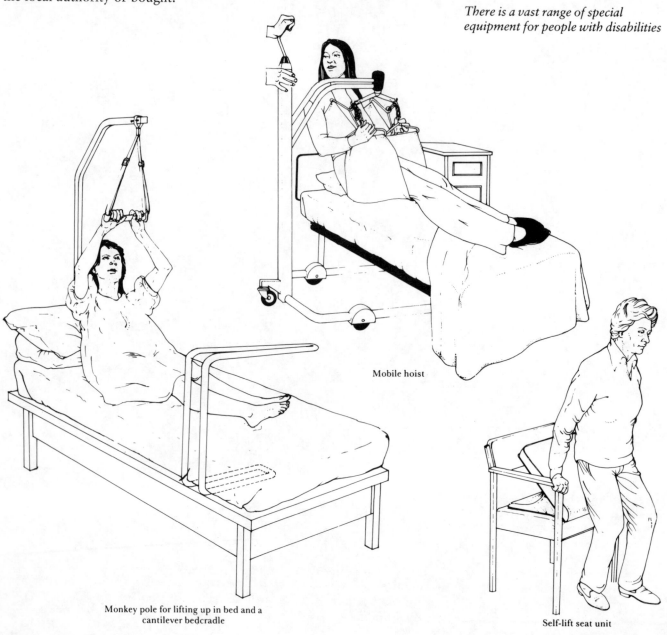

Mobile hoist

Monkey pole for lifting up in bed and a
cantilever bedcradle

Self-lift seat unit

Locations of disabled living centres

Trying out special equipment

Some areas have **Disabled Living Centres**. These centres stock a range of special equipment. They can be visited by people with disabilities and their carers: equipment is demonstrated and can be tried out. Occupational therapists are on hand to give advice and information. The centres may be run by voluntary organisations, by the health service or by social services. There is also a travelling exhibition which tours Scotland.

Finance

Grants are available from social services to pay for major adaptations to homes such as putting in a lift. The family will be expected to contribute to the cost, depending on its income.

Finding out more: aids and adaptations

★ The Disabled Living Foundation provides information on aids and adaptations as well as on other aspects of disability. It offers a number of useful publications, including the leaflet *Aids and Equipment for People with Disabilities*.

5.5 Support for informal carers

Many people are involved in caring for a relative or friend who has a disability or handicap. The pressure on informal carers has increased with the trend away from residential care to care in the community. 'Community care' usually means care by a single relative. Many carers are women. Some carers are themselves elderly or suffering a disability. There are also children who are placed in the caring role, due to the disability of a parent or other relative.

The needs of carers have attracted attention in recent years with newspaper reports and television documentaries highlighting their isolation. Most social services departments are aware of the need to provide support for carers. However, this recognition has not necessarily led to carers' needs being comprehensively met.

Respite care

Most social services departments offer **respite care**, whereby the person being cared for can go into a residential home for short periods. This gives carers a break. An annual programme of respite care may be planned for the client and family.

Day centres have been mentioned (page 94): these may be used to benefit the carer as well as the client. Some local authorities provide **'sitting' schemes** whereby someone will replace the carer in his or her own home. This could allow a carer to get on with tasks such as shopping, or provide time for recreation and social outings. (See also the Crossroads scheme – page 93.)

Mutual support

The Carers' National Association (*Carers*) was formed in 1988 as a result of merging two already existing organisations for carers. This organisation provides advice and information with excellent leaflets on various aspects of caring and a bi-monthly journal. There are also local groups which provide

Carers provide support for people caring for a friend or relative

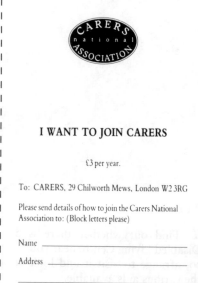

I WANT TO JOIN CARERS

£3 per year.

To: CARERS, 29 Chilworth Mews, London W2 3RG

Please send details of how to join the Carers National Association to: (Block letters please)

Name _____

Address _____

_____

_____

Postcode _____

CASE STUDIES

Imagine that the following people are your clients. What help and advice would you offer them?

(a) Carol is 50. She cares for her mother, who lives with her. Her mother is showing signs of becoming senile. Carol is very reluctant to allow her mother to go into a residential home, but is concerned that she herself cannot cope.

(b) Nick and Jackie have a child with cerebral palsy. Although they have little money to spare, they are desperate to take their three children on holiday.

(c) Allen is 20. As a result of a childhood accident, he is confined to a wheelchair. He wants to go abroad alone, to visit relatives in America. He needs to find out about travel arrangements.

(d) Ivy is 78. She is crippled with arthritis and is finding it difficult to carry out many of the household tasks. Even small things like turning off the cooker taps present a problem.

support and other services. The Carers' National Association also acts as a pressure group, bringing the needs of carers to the attention of the government and other policy-making bodies.

WORDCHECK

voluntary organisation An organisation which has not been set up by a government body and which does not aim to make a profit.
access officers Employees of the local authority, who ensure that public buildings meet the requirements of access for people with disabilities.
home-care service A service which provides personal care, such as help with washing and dressing, in a client's own home.
continence nurse advisor Someone who provides counselling, advice and information for people with problems related to incontinence.
occupational therapist Someone who helps people with disabilities to live a normal life, teaching necessary skills and providing special equipment.
Disabled Living Centre A place where equipment available to help people with disabilities is demonstrated.
respite care Short-term care in a residential home for someone who is otherwise living with relatives or alone in the community.

Finding out more: support for carers

★ *With Due Care and Attention*, by Gillian Parker, summarises research information on carers. The second edition was published in 1990 by the Family Policy Studies Centre.

6 Employment

Unemployment continues to be a serious problem in Britain. Some two million people are currently included in the official statistics. And even this high figure may not represent the true number of unemployed people. The government figure counts only people who are registered as out of work and eligible for benefit. This excludes certain people. One group to be excluded are young people who cannot claim Income Support until they are eighteen. Another excluded group are the women who cannot claim benefit because of their husbands' income. It may well be that the real number of unemployed people is closer to three million.

Unemployment does not hit everyone in the population equally. Like most other things, it is unequally distributed amongst people. The groups of people who are more vulnerable include younger people, who will not be taken on in times of recession, and older people, who find it hard to get new jobs if they are made redundant. Members of ethnic minorities experience discrimination and find it harder to find and keep jobs than do white people. Adults with learning difficulties may find themselves at the bottom of the pile when there is not enough work to go around. Similarly anyone with a less than totally respectable history – such as someone who has been in prison or someone who has spent time in a psychiatric hospital – may be rejected as a matter of course when there are twenty applicants for each job. These people, who may also be the clients of care workers, may need extra advice and help from you in looking for work.

The importance of employment

Helping someone to find a good job can prevent a lot of other problems. Work is very important in our society. Most obviously, it provides an income. Although there are benefits which can be claimed by people without work (see Chapter 4), these are very low and do not provide a very good standard of living. Most people in work are financially better off than people living on benefits.

But the benefits of work are not only financial. Work provides a structure to the day. Days of unemployment are long and slow: people become bored, restless and depressed. Work provides company. For many people, work is the main source of friends. Unemployment is often very lonely. But more than all of this, work can provide a sense of purpose and meaning. It gives status – a sense of *being* someone. This can be seen by the way people's first question on meeting a stranger is often 'What do you do?'

People who are unemployed are more likely to be in poor physical and mental health. Suicides are more common amongst unemployed people. A young person who can find a satisfying job may be prevented from getting into trouble with the police and courts. Adults with learning difficulties are likely to benefit from the opportunity to show what they can do, and from the sense of being part of society that work can give.

TO DO

Survey the local employment opportunities.

- Look in the newspapers at the kinds of work being advertised.
- Visit the Jobcentre. What sorts of jobs are available?
- Are there jobs for people without qualifications? Are there any jobs suitable for adults with learning difficulties? What sorts of rates of pay are being offered?

6.1 Advice and information

Finding out about vacancies

One starting point for someone looking for work is the local **Jobcentre**. The address of the nearest Jobcentre can be found in the phone book. Jobcentres are usually in the centres of towns, so as to be easily accessible for most people. Local job **vacancies** are displayed on cards, and anyone can walk around and see what is available. If a suitable vacancy is found, the staff will arrange an interview with the employer. Jobcentres also provide a range of information and advice and can provide the route into other services (described below). The government has plans to merge Jobcentres with **Unemployment Benefit Offices** and provide both facilities under one roof. These plans should start taking effect in the mid-1990s.

Vacancies are also advertised in local and national newspapers, depending on the type of job. Libraries hold copies of newspapers, which can be looked at free. Specialised journals advertise jobs in particular fields of work, for example the *Nursing Times* is a source of nursing jobs and *Community Care* advertises jobs in social work. There are also private employment agencies: some of these specialise in a particular type of work, others are more general.

Looking for work

When someone first becomes unemployed, he or she will be seen by a **New Client Adviser** at the Jobcentre or the Unemployment Benefit Office. The adviser will discuss the best strategy for finding a job and also advise on benefits. The result of this interview will be a **Back-to-Work Plan**.

If the person is still unemployed after three months, he or she will be offered an interview with a **Claimant Adviser**. Here the Back-to-Work Plan will be reviewed and new actions to find work considered. People who have been unemployed for three months are entitled to attend a **Jobsearch seminar**. This lasts for two days and provides information on how to look for and apply for jobs. Interview techniques are also discussed. People do not lose benefit whilst attending these or any other courses, and fares are paid. For a period of up to four weeks after the seminar, people can drop in for advice and support.

After six months, the unemployed person can attend a **Job Club**. People with disabilities and those who have just finished a youth training scheme or employment training do not have to wait six months. The Job Club again offers advice, information and support. People attending can have the free use of a telephone, newspapers, stationery and stamps in their search for work.

There is also a scheme called the **Job Interview Guarantee** (**JIG**). The qualifications for this are similar to those for the Job Club. This scheme guarantees an interview with a local employer at the end of a week's training in interview and other job-application skills and techniques.

Every six months that someone is unemployed and claiming benefit, he or she will be invited to a **Restart interview**. In this interview the Claimant Advisor will consider the person's position and review the Back-to-Work Plan, and will usually offer one of these possible opportunities:

- job vacancies to apply for;
- a training place (described later in this chapter);

- a place in a Job Club;
- a job interview through the Job Interview Guarantee scheme;
- a one-week Restart course (described below);
- the chance of self-employment with government help.

The idea of **Restart courses** is to give people back the confidence they might have lost after a long period of unemployment; each unsuccessful job application is a knock to morale. The courses are informal and try to meet the needs of the people involved. They look at strengths and skills and try to find new opportunities and ideas for work. Again they provide advice and information on the skills needed in seeking work.

WORDCHECK

New Client Advisor A counsellor at the Jobcentre who provides guidance for people who have become unemployed.

Claimant Advisor A counsellor at the Jobcentre who sees people who have been unemployed for longer than three months.

Back-to-Work Plan A plan for looking for work, drawn up in an interview between an unemployed person and the New Claimant Advisor.

Jobsearch seminar An event planned to help people in techniques for looking for work.

Job Club A service which provides facilities to help people look for work.

Youth Training (YT) Training for young people: those without jobs receive an allowance.

Employment Training (ET) Training for unemployed adults: it pays benefit plus £10 (April 1992).

Job Interview Guarantee (JIG) A week's training in applying for jobs, with an interview with a local employer at the end.

Restart interview For people who have been unemployed for over six months; an interview to review the Back-to-Work Plan.

Restart course A course for unemployed people, to improve their confidence and job-searching skills.

Finding out more: looking for work

★ The Employment Service provides a booklet which describes the various schemes for unemployed people. It is called *Just the Job*, and is available from Jobcentres or from the Employment Service.

★ The Employment Service also publishes a set of leaflets designed to help people looking for work:

- *Get that Job* contains tips and guidance on looking for work, applying for jobs and doing interviews.
- *Be Your Own Boss* describes ways of being self-employed and has addresses for further information.
- *Getting Back to Work* has advice and ideas for older people who are looking for work.

6.2 The Careers Service

Local authorities must provide careers advice for all young people at school. Careers officers visit schools, offering careers guidance and making young people aware of opportunities for employment and training. The local careers office also acts as an employment agency for young people aged between 16 and 18. It has training schemes on offer and liaises with local employers to keep tabs on the local job market.

The Careers Service has no statutory obligation to older people – no legislation requires that it provide a service for adults. However, most areas offer some form of adult guidance service. Anyone can contact this service for advice and information and to arrange a careers interview.

Colleges and universities also have their own careers advisors.

6.3 Training and educational opportunities

The government has set up eighty-two **Training and Enterprise Councils** (TECs) across the country. These are led by local business people and aim to meet local training needs. They provide a number of different services.

Training and work experience

TECs run programmes of training and work experience for young people. These are aimed at all 16- and 17-year-olds not in school. Places are guaranteed to those who want them. Some people who are a little older are still entitled to a place if they were unable to have one earlier for reasons such as disability or pregnancy. Training is available for those in work as well as those without jobs. Young people who are not working receive a training allowance. Some people also qualify for help with travel, lodgings and other costs.

TECs also offer training for adults. In most cases this is for people who have been unemployed for at least six months. There are exceptions to this: people with a disability; those whose first language is not English and who need language training; women returning to work after looking after a family; and people who have been in prison. The scheme is called **Employment Training** (ET), and it usually lasts for up to 12 months. Employment Training programmes are intended to meet the needs of the individual and a training advisor works with the person to design a suitable programme. This could include work experience, training and education. People on ET receive their normal benefits plus £10 (April 1992). There is help with travel costs over £4. Single parents who place a child with a minder or in a nursery can claim child-care costs.

Loans to finance courses

Career-development loans (CDLs) are available to help people pay for a course they wish to attend. The loan can be from £300 to £5000 (April 1992). It covers 80 per cent of the fees, and all the expenses of books and other materials. The course must be work-related and must last longer than one week but no longer than a year. Three months after the end of the course, the person will have to start paying back the loan.

If the course is full-time, it is likely to affect the person's availability for work and therefore make him or her ineligible for benefit.

Open learning

A relatively recent innovation is **open learning**. This means that students can learn at their own pace, in their own time and without having to attend a college. A package of learning materials is provided, perhaps including books, videos and computer programmes. Sometimes there are support groups. There is a *Directory of Open Learning* which lists the courses that are available. This can be found in libraries. The Open College and the Open University provide college and university courses through **distance learning**.

Colleges

Unemployed people can also enrol on courses at local colleges of further and adult education. Further education colleges are more likely to offer work-related or academic courses leading to qualifications. Adult education colleges are more likely to offer recreational study. This distinction does not always hold true, however: in practice there is a lot of overlap between the two types of colleges.

Some colleges may offer courses specifically for unemployed people. But unemployed people can also join more general courses. Most colleges will offer some kind of reduction in price for people on benefit. Some courses may be free. Grants are also available from the county council. These may cover fees and in some cases other costs as well. Colleges may have a special fund to help people in financial difficulty – perhaps with the cost of books or travel. All these things are worth asking about. Most colleges have student welfare offices which can advise on these and other issues.

ET leaflet for unemployed adults

The effect on benefits

People on Income Support can usually study part-time without losing their benefit. This is a concession known as the **21-Hour Rule**. Because it is a concession it may be applied differently in different areas.

The way the rule tends to work is that someone can study at a college without losing benefit provided that the course is no more than 21 hours per week. This does not include study at home. The course must not be one designated by the college as a full-time course: full-time students cannot claim benefit.

The situation is slightly different for someone claiming Unemployment Benefit. The rules here are that the person must be available for work on each day that benefit is claimed. Claimants must be looking for work during each week they claim benefit.

WORDCHECK

Training and Education Councils (TECs) Councils in each area, led by local business people, which aim to meet local training needs.

Youth Training (YT) Training for young people: those without jobs receive an allowance.

Employment Training (ET) Training for unemployed adults: it pays benefit plus £10 (April 1992).

career-development loans Loans for training related to work.

open learning Self-study packages which enable people to study without attending a centre.

21-Hour Rule A concession whereby people on benefits can attend college part-time.

Finding out more: training for unemployed people

★   Contact the local Training and Enterprise Council (TEC) to discover the local opportunities for training. If the address and phone number are not in the phone book, ask at the local Jobcentre.

★   There may be a computerised database with information on training and educational opportunities. It is called **Training Access Points (TAP)** and may be available in the Jobcentre or library.

Finding out more: study while unemployed

★   Three useful publications for unemployed people wanting to study are published by the Unemployment Unit and Youthaid. These are:

- *Studying on the Dole*;
- *Signing On and Actively Seeking Work*;
- *Restart: Where You Stand*.

TO FIND OUT

1   Check whether the local library has open-learning materials which can be borrowed.

2   Write to the Open College to find out what is on offer.

TO FIND OUT

Contact local colleges of adult and further education. Find out what is available.

- Are there reductions in fees for people who are unemployed?
- Are there any courses specifically for unemployed people?
- Which courses fit the 21-Hour Rule for people who are on Income Support and cannot afford to lose their benefit?

6.4 Starting a new business

Training and Enterprise Councils (TECs) can provide advice and assistance for people wishing to start a new business. Several things are available.

First, there are **Enterprise Awareness events.** These are usually for one day and encourage people who are interested in setting up a business to think about what is involved.

Business advice and counselling are available to provide support in getting going with a new business. There is a free **planning kit** which helps people to design a plan to put to a bank manager or other lender and to avoid unnecessary risks. Short, part-time courses are available to train people in the various skills needed to set up and run a business.

Finally, people may be entitled to an **Enterprise Allowance.** This gives an income until the business gets going. Local TECs decide how long the grant should be for and the amount to be paid. People have to have been unemployed for a while to qualify. A wide variety of schemes have been funded in this way in the past, including counselling services and alternative health care.

Details of all these schemes can be obtained from Jobcentres.

6.5 Help with interview expenses

People who have been unemployed for four months or more can in some cases claim expenses for travel to an interview. This help is only available if the travel is more than a normal daily travelling distance. The expenses covered include an overnight stay if this is necessary.

If someone feels he or she needs new clothes to attend an interview, it might be worth applying to the Social Fund for a loan.

6.6 People with disabilities – extra help

People with disabilities can make use of any of the schemes already described in this chapter. There is also some extra help available. The **Disablement Resettlement Officer (DRO)** can give advice and support in finding work. The **Disablement Advisory Service (DAS)** provides help for people with disabilities in work, and helps people reach their full potential after an accident or illness. The DAS also works with employers to improve employment opportunities for people with disabilities.

There are a number of special services available to help people with disabilities.

Assessment and rehabilitation

The aim of **assessment** is to look at the person and his or her situation and to find the most suitable kind of work. **Rehabilitation** aims to improve people's confidence and skills, and prepare them for work or perhaps retraining.

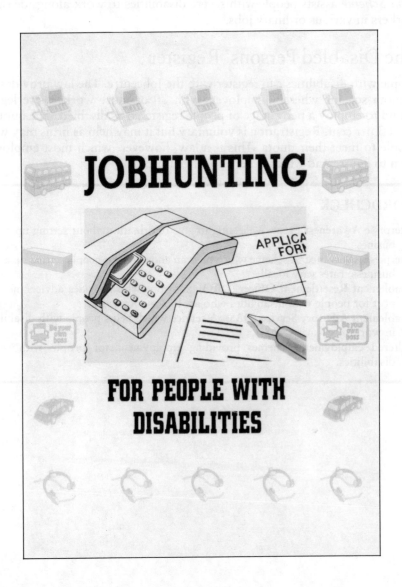

Leaflet providing special help for people with disabilities

Special aids to employment

If people need special equipment in order to work, this can be borrowed free of charge.

Assistance with fares to work

Where people cannot use public transport because of a disability, a grant can be claimed to pay the extra costs. The maximum is £87.50 a week (April 1992).

Personal reader service

Visually handicapped people can claim money to pay a part-time reader.

Sheltered employment

This is for people with more severe disabilities. There are special workshops run by a government organisation called *Remploy*. Local authorities and voluntary organisations also run sheltered workshops. The *Sheltered Placement Scheme* assists people with severe disabilities to work alongside other workers in various ordinary jobs.

The Disabled Persons' Register

People with disabilities can register with the Jobcentre. The law provides for a quota scheme whereby employers with 20 or more workers are legally bound to employ a percentage of people registered as disabled. The quota is set at 3 per cent. Registration is voluntary but it may help as firms may want people to meet their quota. This is a law, however, which most employers seem to ignore and which is very poorly enforced.

WORDCHECK

Enterprise Awareness event A meeting to give information about setting up a new business.
Enterprise Allowance A scheme which pays an allowance to people setting up a new business; rates vary locally.
Disablement Resettlement Officer (DRO) Someone who provides advice and support for people with disabilities who are looking for work.
Disablement Advisory Service (DAS) A service which helps people with disabilities in work.
sheltered employment Schemes providing employment for people with severe disabilities.

TO DO

Survey one or two local employers to find out their policies on employing people with disabilities.

- Do they currently employ people with disabilities?
- Do they have any extra facilities?
- Would they consider someone with a disability?

6.7 Voluntary work

The emphasis in this chapter is on *paid* employment, but **voluntary work** is an important alternative to paid employment. A voluntary job can provide the same meaning in a person's life as a paid job. Voluntary work gives a sense of purpose and worth, a structure to the day, and social contact with others. Voluntary work is also a way of developing skills and confidence.

Many organisations are desperate for volunteers and it is much easier to find voluntary work than to find a paid job. Many different types of activities are available in many different kinds of settings. There is a much greater likelihood therefore of finding something which fits an individual's particular needs, talents and interests. Hours and times are usually flexible. Many organisations are able to pay expenses and a few pay a little more than this.

Many people who do voluntary work are past retirement age and there is no prejudice about age in the voluntary sector. Similarly, less weight is attached to qualifications and experience than in the competition for paid employment. Voluntary organisations are less likely than many employers to discriminate against someone with a history of mental illness. Although many organisations – especially those involving children – carry out a police check on applicants, this does not mean they will not accept someone with a criminal record. Some people use voluntary work as a way of returning to paid employment, perhaps as a means of gradual return after an illness, or a method of gaining experience. Using voluntary work to gain experience for work or training is especially common in the field of social work. Some voluntary organisations provide training courses for their volunteers, and these may lead on to NVQ and other qualifications.

Voluntary work gives a sense of purpose and worth

There are several ways of finding out about voluntary work. Most towns have a **Volunteer Bureau** or **Community Volunteer Service** centre, which acts as a sort of clearing house, fitting volunteers to particular needs. The address and phone number for this should be in the phone book. Alternatively, voluntary organisations sometimes advertise in local papers, and the library probably has a noticeboard for voluntary organisations and may keep a list of all such organisations.

CASE STUDIES

Imagine you have clients in the following situations. What advice, help and support could you offer?

(a) Mary has not worked since her children were born. Now the youngest has left home, she feels her life to be very empty. She is getting depressed. The doctor is reluctant to prescribe drugs and suggests she get a job.

(b) Tony is 20. He has not worked since he left school, and has been cautioned by police when involved with a group of young men caught trying to break into a shop.

(c) As a result of an accident at work, Harvinder cannot walk. He cannot return to his previous employment, and he cannot stand the idea of doing nothing for the rest of his life. He is 40 years old.

(d) Sheila is a widow who has just retired from a lifetime working, as a schoolteacher and later as a headteacher. Having looked forward to retirement, she now feels lonely and worthless.

7 Children

This chapter looks at the welfare provision which exists to help children. This involves looking at some rather diverse aspects of social policy and welfare provision.

The involvement of the State

It is often said that this is a country which has no real policy on children and very little provision. Children tend to be seen as the responsibility of their parents and the government intervenes only to fill the gaps. This can be clearly seen in the first area which this chapter looks at, that of **day-care** provision for children. Parents are very much left to solve their own problems, with the authorities taking a minimal role in registering people who provide day care. Most day care for working parents is provided by relatives or by private **childminders**. The only time the government has been seriously involved in providing day care has been in wartime, when women have been needed to work in jobs left vacant by the men at war.

Day care can be an important part of a package to help a family. You may see day care as a means of preventing family problems and ultimately of keeping a child out of care. For a mother trying to keep her head above water in difficult circumstances, day care may be an essential lifeline. It gives her vital space for herself or for the other children in the family. Some forms of social services provision take a different approach, aiming to work with the child and parents together. **Family centres** expect parents to attend and work on such areas as parenting skills. You may seek day care for a client where a child has special needs. Specially trained staff can help a child develop his or her full potential. Day care also plays an important part in working with families where there is a risk of **child abuse**. Workers are trained to spot signs of abuse and can also give early warnings of other problems relating to a child's emotional, intellectual or physical development, thereby helping to keep a family together.

Children in danger

The second section of this chapter looks at the protection of children in danger. This is an area which has received a lot of media attention in recent years. There have been a number of very controversial cases and consequent pressure on the government to change the law.

Child abuse is something of a no-win area for social workers. There is still a strong feeling that the family is a private area and that social workers should not interfere. In some of the controversial cases, social workers have been blamed for being too quick to suspect abuse and to remove children from their homes. On the other hand, social workers are also blamed when a child dies from abuse. When they don't react quickly and decisively, they are seen as gullible and too soft on the parents.

The 1989 Children Act

In 1989 a new Children Act was passed. This is an important piece of legislation which covers many aspects of children's welfare. It includes new rules on day-care provision, a new approach to sharing child care after divorce, and a lot of new procedures concerning the protection of children in danger. There are also new rules for children being looked after by the local authority or in care.

The 1989 Children Act tries to give greater rights to children. It also tries to balance parents' rights with the powers needed by the local authorities to protect children from abuse and neglect. The law acknowledges the importance of families, and requires the local authorities always to work with the family and to maintain links between children and family members.

7.1 Day care for children

There is a growing need for day care for children. Clients may want day care for a variety of reasons. More women are wanting paid employment, even when their children are small. Women who do not have paid jobs still feel that their children benefit from the different experiences they have in nurseries and playgroups. Families are smaller these days, and many children do not have sisters or brothers to play with at home. Nurseries and playgroups have bigger and more varied toys than many parents could afford. They can allow messy and wet play without worrying about the housework involved. Many of the staff are trained in play methods and in child development. They may have more imaginative ideas for play. Nurseries and playgroups also play an important role in preparing children for school. Children will have experienced leaving their parents for short periods and be used to a different environment and to a day which is more structured than at home.

This country provides less in the way of day care than do many other European countries. As a result much of the provision is privately offered – mostly by childminders, working in their own homes. Although many parents use childminders, this is not their preferred option. Workplace or other nurseries are more popular. But these are few and far between. Where they do exist, they are often too expensive for parents to afford. This section examines the various types of child care available.

The duties of local authorities

Provision of child care

Although local authorities do not have to meet all parents' needs for child care, they do have certain duties in this area. The 1989 Children Act states that local authority social services departments, in association with local education authorities, must review day-care services for children under the age of 8. This includes services provided by the local authority as well as those provided by childminders and other private and voluntary organisations. The review must be carried out at least every three years and the results published.

The Act also gives local authorities the duty to provide day-care services for children in need. This includes children up to 5, and those up to 16 after school hours and in the school holidays. Need is defined in two ways. It includes children with disabilities; and children who are unlikely to achieve or maintain a reasonable standard of health and development, or who would not do so without special provision. Examples of services could be day nurseries, places in playgroups, a place with a childminder or an out-of-school club. Local authorities may provide services for other children as well, but the government does not require them to do so.

Registration of child-care services

The other major responsibility of the local authority social services department in this area is the **registration** of private and voluntary child-care services. Anyone who provides day care for children up to the age of 8 for more than two hours a day must be registered. This includes shared nannies, employed by more than two families.

Before the childminder, nursery or playgroup can be registered, the social services department must decide on their 'fitness'. This has two aspects. First, the minder must be a 'fit' person to care for children, as must any other person living or working on the premises. Secondly, the premises themselves must also be fit.

The Department of Health will issue guidance on what might be looked at in terms of 'fitness'. For the minder, it is likely to include experience, qualifications and multicultural awareness. The local authority will set conditions such as the number of children allowed in the group or to be minded; safety measures which must be taken; and details of required record-keeping. Other conditions can be added. The authority must inspect at least once a year. Fees are charged for this at a rate set by the government.

The 1989 Children Act emphasised the need for an anti-racist and multicultural approach to child care. Registration can be cancelled if the care given to an individual child is thought to be seriously inadequate in terms of the child's religion, racial origin, or cultural and linguistic background.

Finding out more: day care

★   For statistical information on day-care facilities for children, see *Caring for Children: the 1990 report*, by Bromwen Cohen, published by the Family Policy Studies Centre. The Centre also has a number of other publications with information concerning children and families.

★   *Working Mother: a practical handbook*, by Marianne Velmans and Sarah Litvinoff, published by Pathway Press in 1987, has a great deal of information about the practical issues in finding child care, as well as a lot of other information for working parents.

Day nurseries

There are places in **day nurseries** for about 2 per cent of all children under the age of 5. Many local authorities provide day nurseries, but the type of provision varies a great deal from area to area.

In some large towns day care is provided for working parents. In other places the service is in the form of **family centres**. Family centres do not usually take children if the parents are working and places are allocated on the basis of need. The children who are accepted will have special needs or be thought to be at risk or deprived in some way.

There are also nurseries that are run privately. These tend to be expensive. Some employers provide **workplace nurseries** for their staff. It is predicted that this form of provision might increase in the future as employers try to attract women workers. Universities and colleges sometimes provide nursery facilities also, for staff and students. These college and workplace nurseries are popular since only one journey is involved each day for the parent and the child, and the child is close by and can be visited at lunchtimes.

Nurseries are usually open long hours, to accommodate working parents.

Childminders

Childminders are legally required to register with the local authority. Although it is hard to estimate figures, it is likely however that there are people minding who are *not* registered. The delays sometimes put people off; so does the fear that they might be refused registration, or limited in the number of children they can take.

There has been a recent increase in the numbers of childminders. This has put a considerable strain on social services resources. Long waiting lists for registration are common. More pressure will result from the 1989 Children Act, which brought in the need for childminders with children under the age of 8 to register. (Previously the age was 5.)

Most childminders work privately, although a few local authorities have salaried childminders working for them. More commonly, some children will be subsidised by the local authority. Childminders are usually women with young children of their own who want a way of earning extra money without going out to work. Social services hold lists of registered childminders which can be used by someone looking for a childminder.

Standards of childminding vary tremendously, from women who provide excellent care to those with poor facilities and little understanding of children's needs. Some local authorities provide training and support groups for childminders, but this is fairly minimal. There is a national organisation for childminders which provides information and support.

One of the few things available to all childminders is free milk: registered childminders are entitled to receive one-third of a pint of milk per day for each child minded.

Finding out more: childminding

★ For information on childminding, contact the *National Childminding Association*. The Association has local groups which share ideas and provide support. Membership entitles childminders to an insurance policy and a newsletter. NCMA also provides advice and information and leaflets.

Playgroups

About half of all children aged 3 or 4 attend **playgroups**. They usually attend two or three sessions a week for a couple of hours only. Since the hours are so short, parents cannot use playgroups as a means of child care to allow them to work. Some children are however taken to playgroups by their childminders.

Playgroups have to register with social services, who usually expect playgroup supervisors to have had some training. Training is on a part-time basis: it is provided by the *Pre-School Playgroups Association* (PPA), but financed by the county council. The majority of playgroups are affiliated to the PPA. Playgroups encourage parents to be involved, and many of the helpers are parents of playgroup children. Many playgroups will take children with special needs and sometimes social services provide extra support in these cases.

Finding out more: playgroups

★ For information on playgroups, contact the *Pre-School Playgroups Association*. It provides information on playgroups and on starting a playgroup. Through a system of regional and area fieldworkers, the PPA supports local playgroups.

Nursery schools and classes

About a quarter of 3- and 4-year-olds attend a **nursery school** or **nursery class**. Most of the children are in their pre-school year and most attend

Most playgroups are part of the Pre-School Playgroups Association

TO DO

Survey clients on their preferences for child care. Compare working and non-working parents.

Ask about the child care used currently and in the past, and ask people what they would actually *like* to be available.

part-time – either mornings or afternoons. Although the emphasis in nursery schools is still on play, the time is likely to be more structured than in a playgroup, to prepare the children for school.

Many children attend playgroups

Care for school-age children

For working parents, the problem of child care does not end when the child starts school at 5. Very few jobs fit in exactly with school hours and holidays. Most children of working parents are cared for by relatives or childminders. There are, however, a few out-of-school schemes for children after school hours and in the holidays. These usually use the school premises, and tend to be found in large cities.

TO FIND OUT

What facilities are there for child care in your local area?

- Does the local authority provide any day nurseries? If so, on what basis are children accepted?
- Are there any private nurseries?
- Do any local employers provide child care?
- Does the local college have a crèche?
- Find out from social services how many childminders there are in the area. Contact one or two, to compare the costs.
- What playgroups are there? What ages of children do they take? Would they take children with learning difficulties? With disabilities?
- Are there any nursery schools? Which primary schools have nursery classes?
- Are there any facilities for school-age children after school and in the holidays?

CASE STUDIES

Imagine you have clients in the following situations. What help, advice and support would you offer?

(a)   Shelley is 17 and unmarried. She lives alone in a flat with her 1-year-old baby. She loves the baby and has coped so far, but now the child is becoming more active she is finding things more difficult. She is lonely in her flat and showing signs of depression.

(b)   Clare and Stephen's third child, Peter, has Down's syndrome. Sally is very protective of Peter and does not allow any rough-and-tumble play. The others in the family, including Tom, seem jealous of the amount of attention Sally gives to Peter.

(c)   Wendy abused her first child, who is now with foster parents. She is about to give birth to her second child. Her circumstances are now different, in that the father of the second child is supportive. Wendy is frightened that she will lose this child and wants help.

7.2 The law protecting children

The 1989 Children Act aimed to pull together several older Acts and to simplify the law. Under the Act, local authorities have a duty to protect children in their area. This duty is carried out by the social workers in the social services departments. Although the law does not say how local authorities must organise their service, they are bound to provide services which prevent children from being the victims of ill-treatment or neglect. If it is suspected that a child may be in danger, the local authority is bound, under law, to investigate the situation.

There are also voluntary organisations working in the area of child protection. The *National Society for the Prevention of Cruelty to Children* (NSPCC) plays an important role in this area. Its inspectors work in a similar way to social services social workers, often in close liaison. They can be involved in all the court proceedings described below. *Childline* is a telephone helpline for children themselves if they are in trouble. Calls are free and are answered by trained counsellors.

The law

The law provides for a number of different **court orders** which give social workers powers to intervene in families. An aim of the law is to balance the interests of parents, children and the authorities – whilst always having the welfare of the child as the *first* consideration.

In a situation where social workers are concerned for the welfare of a child, they do not *have* to take the child into care. The social worker may feel that it would be damaging for a child to be taken from his or her home. If the child is not felt to be in danger, he or she may be left at home. Social services can provide support in the home – perhaps the services of a family home help, or the support of a social worker. They can also provide money if this will help the situation. The law also provides that help – in the form of different housing, for instance – could be given to someone else in the household, for example someone who is suspected of abusing the child. But these decisions must always be made with the *child's* interests and safety as the main consideration.

Childline is a telephone helpline for children in trouble

Child assessment order

If the social workers feel that a child is at risk at home they must investigate the situation. They must then apply for one of the court orders available or decide to review the situation at a later date.

There have been situations in the past where social workers have not been able to get access to examine a child they were worried about. To stop this happening again, there is now a **child assessment order**. The court will give this order if it feels that there is a suspicion of significant harm to the child, but no immediate emergency. A child assessment order lasts for seven days. It can include the child being taken from the home for examination if this is thought to be necessary.

Emergency protection order

An **emergency protection order** can be granted if the court feels that the child is likely to suffer significant harm if he or she is left at home or allowed to go home. It lasts for seven days and can be extended for a further seven days. The police have the power to remove a child straightaway, but they must then inform the local authority. This is for a period of 72 hours, and the parents must be allowed to see the child.

Care order

A **care order** brings the child into the care of the local authority. It gives parental responsibility for the child to the local authority. With a care order the child would normally be removed from home: the child may live with foster parents or in a community home run by the local authority or a voluntary organisation. (A *supervision order* – see below – is similar but allows the child to remain at home.)

The fact that the local authority has parental responsibility does not remove responsibility from the parents (or the people looking after the child). It is the *prime* responsibility only that goes to the local authority. The law encourages parents to continue to be involved with the child, and local authorities are expected to look for ways to share responsibility. The grounds for a care order or a supervision order are:

- that the child is suffering or is likely to suffer significant harm; *and*
- that the harm is because *either* (a) the care given by the parents is not what it is reasonable to expect, *or* (b) the child is beyond the control of the parents.

Supervision order

With a **supervision order**, the child remains at home and has a social worker whose role is to advise, help and befriend. The child and the parent must make sure the social worker is aware of any moves of house and can meet the child. It may be that the child is required to live at a particular place or has to join in some organised activities.

Interim care order

It is also possible for an **interim care order** to be made, if the full hearing cannot take place for some reason. This lasts for up to eight weeks, and a second one can only last for four weeks.

Guardian ad litem

There is a system whereby an adult is appointed to represent the interests of the child in court. This person is called a **guardian *ad litem***. It is the duty of the court to appoint such a person unless the court is satisfied that it is not necessary to do so. The guardian *ad litem* carries out an investigation, interviewing various people such as the child himself or herself, social workers, parents and relatives. A report is then presented to the court which tries to state what actions are in the best interests of the child.

Case conferences

As was mentioned earlier, the law does not state how the social services departments must act to prevent child abuse. The usual system is through multi-disciplinary committees and **case conferences**. These bring together all the different people who might be involved with a particular child. Knowledge is shared and a decision made as to the best course of action. The

Case conferences bring together all the people involved with a particular child

people involved are likely to include social workers, police officers, a member of staff from the school, GPs, and other health-care workers such as health visitors. There may also be workers from the National Society for Prevention of Cruelty to Children if they also are involved with the case.

'At risk' registers

Each area keeps a register of children who have been abused or who are suspected of having been abused. This is looked after either by the local authority or by the NSPCC.

Other local authority involvement

It is possible for a child to be looked after by the local authority without being in care. This happens in situations where the local authority is providing a home for a child without there being a court order. Social services must provide for children who have no one to look after them, who are lost or abandoned, or whose carer is unable – temporarily or permanently – to provide care. The child's wishes in such a situation should be considered and the parents are allowed to take the child back without any notice.

The local authority has a duty to help contact between the parents and the child. This can include paying the costs of visits to the child. There must also be regular reviews of the situations of all children being looked after by the local authority.

WORDCHECK

voluntary organisation An organisation which has not been set up by a government body and which does not aim to make a profit.

helpline A telephone counselling or information service.

child assessment order A court order which allows social workers access to a child whom they suspect might be being abused.

emergency protection order A court order which gives social workers the right to remove a child who is felt to be in danger.

care order A court order which brings a child into the care of the local authority.

supervision order A court order whereby a child lives at home but has a social worker as advisor and counsellor.

interim care order A temporary care order when a full court hearing is not possible.

guardian *ad litem* An adult who represents a vulnerable person's interests in the court.

case conference A multi-disciplinary meeting to share ideas about a social work case.

'at risk' register A list of children who are thought to be at risk of child abuse.

Finding out more: the 1989 Children Act

★ A number of organisations have produced guides to the 1989 Children Act. Recommended guides include:

- *An Introduction to the Children Act* by the Department of Health (London: HMSO, 1989).
- *Blackstone's Guide to the Children Act 1989*, a detailed and comprehensive guide by Bridge, Bridge and Luke (Blackstone Press, 1989).
- *Working with the Children Act 1989*, from the National Children's Bureau.
- Community Care produced a 20-page guide to the Act which can be obtained by writing to *Guide to the Children Act* (Orders) at Community Care.

7.3 Provision for children in need

Services for children in need are provided by social services departments and by voluntary and private organisations. In the future it is likely that the services will more commonly be run by private and voluntary organisations. Social services will monitor and use the services run by independent organisations. Facilities such as children's homes which are currently owned and run by social services may be turned over to independent organisations.

Social services vary from area to area in the provision they make for children in need of support or care. It is however a general policy that where possible children should be cared for in a family environment. Gone are the days of large institutional orphanages. So the first aim would be for a child to be cared for in his or her own home, perhaps with the support of family home helps and social workers. There are also various day centres which provide counselling, therapy and support.

Foster parents

If the child could not remain with his or her immediate family or with relatives, **foster parents** would be looked for. These are people, not necessarily trained, who care for children in their own home. This may be a short-term or a long-term arrangement. Foster parents who apply are carefully vetted. If accepted, they are paid an allowance for each child in their care. Fostering does not always work out: it is quite common for fostering arrangements to break down, especially with older or very disturbed children. Entering a new family can be a very emotionally demanding and stressful situation for a child. Voluntary organisations such as *Barnardo's* also run fostering schemes, sometimes specialising in working with children with special needs.

Residential accommodation

Sometimes a family situation is not possible or suitable for a child. In such a case the child can be placed in **residential accommodation**. Social services homes for children are usually small, and appear very much like ordinary houses. They are run by **house parents** and a team of other staff. The staff will probably not live on the premises but there will be facilities for staff to sleep over at nights. There are children's homes run by voluntary organisations, too, such as the *National Children's Homes* (NCH). Private organisations also run children's homes, and these are used by social services departments when necessary.

Other services

Social services and voluntary organisations may provide various other services such as day centres and support services. **Child-guidance clinics** are usually administered by the local education authority. The staff working in the clinics are employed by various different authorities, however: there will be **social workers** from the social services department, and **psychotherapists** and **psychiatrists** from the health authority. **Educational psychologists** may also work in the clinic. Child-guidance clinics work with children and families where there are emotional problems. The work is usually long-term, with weekly meetings.

TO FIND OUT

1 Contact the county council or the local social services department to find out what the local policy is on caring for children in need.

2 What services are offered locally for children and young people? Start with social services, but consider also any privately-run facilities or those offered by voluntary organisations.

WORDCHECK

voluntary organisation An organisation which has not been set up by a government body and which does not aim to make a profit.

child-guidance clinic A service which provides therapy and counselling for families and children with emotional and psychological problems.

Finding out more: Barnardo's

★ *Barnardo's* provides a number of services for children in need. It runs a fostering service and specialises in working with children with learning difficulties. It has residential centres and hostels. It supports young people and families in the community, and has day-care centres for under-5s.

7.4 Young offenders

In law a child has to be 10 before he or she can commit a crime. If a child aged between 10 and 14 commits a crime, it must be shown to the court that the child knew that what he or she was doing was wrong. Between the ages of 14 and 16 a child is capable of committing a crime, but will be classed as a **juvenile** and dealt with under the juvenile justice system.

Young offenders appear before the **juvenile court**. This may be in the same building as the magistrate's court, but it is otherwise quite separate and there are different principles and rules. The main principle is that the welfare of the child must be considered as well as the offence. Children are seen as products of their home and social environment, and as in need of help rather than punishment. The court will receive reports from social workers and probation officers. These people look at the home and family, report on schooling, and examine many other aspects of the child's personality and life. Social workers play an important role in working with young offenders. As well as producing reports for the court, they are responsible for supervision orders (see below). They work with young offenders to try to prevent re-offending. In some areas this work is done through **juvenile justice centres**. These provide a range of activities to help young people in trouble.

The police usually deal with juveniles through their **Community Services Branch** (CSB). They also follow a special code when dealing with young offenders. This requires that 'the appropriate adult' be contacted and be present when a young offender is being interviewed. The appropriate adult would normally be a parent, but could be a social worker or some other person.

In some cases, the police will **caution** a young person whom they have caught committing a crime. This is a serious and formal warning which prevents the young person from getting into the justice system. A previous caution can be mentioned if a young person is later sentenced for a subsequent offence. A caution can only be given if the young person admits to the crime and if the parents agree to this procedure.

The police deal with juveniles through their Community Services Branch

Community service can be used as an alternative to custody

Finding out more: rights at police stations

★   For more detailed information on rights at police stations and other aspects of the law, see *Law for Social Workers* by Hugh Brayne and Gerry Martin (Blackstone Press: second edition, 1991).

The juvenile court

The courts have a number of options when considering the case of a young offender. As mentioned earlier, the court will look at the whole situation – not just the offence – in deciding the best course of action. For example, it would be possible for several youngsters involved in the same offence each to receive different treatment. The rest of this section lists the various options open to the juvenile court.

Custody

A custodial sentence is one in which a young person is sent to a **detention centre** or a **borstal**. This is the most serious sentence the court can give. The young person must be aged 14 or over in the case of a boy and 15 or over in the case of a girl. It can only be given if the offence is one for which an older person would be sent to prison. Also it must be the case that the young person has already had other forms of punishment in the community which have not succeeded in stopping him or her re-offending.

The court will not give this kind of sentence unless it feels that to give another non-custodial sentence would do no good. The court must also feel that such a sentence is necessary in view of the seriousness of the offence or the need to protect the public. In other words, sending a young person to a detention centre is a last resort. It would not happen in the case of a first offence.

Community service order

Under a **community service order** the offender must spend some time working in the community. The young person must be 16 and must agree to the order. As with custody, the crime must be one for which an adult would be imprisoned. The minimum amount of time which can be given is 40 hours and the maximum is 120 hours.

Fine

A young offender can be fined. The maximum **fine** for a 10–13-year-old is £100 and the maximum for a 14–16-year-old is £400 (April 1992). The court will look at the young person's ability to pay – the child's, rather than the parents – and the fine can be paid in instalments.

Supervision order

This means the offender must work with a supervisor from social services or the probation service. The role of the supervisor is to befriend and advise.

The supervision order can last up to three years. Restrictions can be attached. These include having to live in local authority accommodation, having to live with a particular person (usually a relative), having to join in supervised activities, and being prevented from going out at certain times. This last – a **curfew** – may, for example, prevent someone who has caused trouble at football matches from attending football matches. The restrictions can apply only for the first 90 days.

Recognisance

This means that a parent or guardian agrees to control the young person. A sum of money is agreed – to a maximum of £1000 – which will be forfeited if the young person commits a further crime. There is a maximum period of three years, and the order cannot go past the young person's 18th birthday.

Attendance centre

This is another decision which can be made only if the crime is one for which an adult could be imprisoned. And, unless there are special circumstances, this cannot be given to a young person who has already been in a borstal or detention centre. The young offender must turn up at the attendance centre for a period of between 12 and 24 hours. Attendance centres are usually run by the police and held in schools or youth clubs. Commonly, they are held for two hours each Saturday.

Deferred sentence

If something is about to change in the offender's life – perhaps a new job or a change of school – the court may decide to delay making a decision until afterwards. The delay can only be for six months and the young person must agree with the plan.

Discharge

It is possible for the court to decide that no punishment is appropriate. An **absolute discharge** means that the offence is ignored for all purposes except sentencing for any *future* offence. A **conditional discharge** can be given for up to three years. If the person commits a further offence, he or she will be sentenced for the original offence *as well as* the later one which the court is then considering.

Compensation order

The offender can be told to **compensate** the victim of the crime. This can be the only punishment, or it can be given with other sentences. Account must be taken of the young person's ability to pay.

WORDCHECK

juvenile court The court which deals with young offenders.

supervision order A court order whereby a child lives at home but has a social worker as advisor and counsellor.

Community Services Branch (CSB) A branch of the police which deals with young people and others thought to be vulnerable.

caution A formal warning given by the police, without a case going to court.

community service order A sentence which means that the offender has to work in the community for a set number of hours.

recognisance A court order which requires parents or guardians to control a young offender.

attendance centre Provision for young offenders, usually run by the police on Saturdays.

deferred sentence Sentencing is delayed until a specified date.

absolute discharge No sentence is given.

conditional discharge An offender will be sentenced for the given offence only if he or she commits another offence.

compensation order A court order which requires an offender to compensate the victim of the crime.

TO DO

Think about the following situations and decide what you think the police or the court should do. If you think you need more information, what do you want to know?

Make the decision first using the list of possible options open to the court (pages 127–9). Then consider whether there is anything you would rather decide, if you were free to impose *any* punishment or treatment.

(a)   A boy of 10 steals a toy from a shop. The home situation is that his mother and father have recently split up. The child does not show any sign of being particularly upset by this, however.

(b)   Three boys, aged 10, 12 and 15, burn down a barn. The 15-year-old has already been to court for a similar offence and is currently going to an attendance centre. His parents are divorced and he lives with his father. The father is rarely at home: he works shifts and likes to go to the pub when he is not working nights. The other two are brothers and have no previous history of offending. They have recently moved to the area. Their parents seem to look after them well.

(c)   Two boys of 16 attack and injure another boy of the same age. The boy who is attacked is white and has been insulting and bullying younger Asian children in school. The boys who injure him are Asian. None of the boys has any previous history of offending. The Asians are successful in school and about to start A-levels; the white boy is regarded by the school as a troublemaker.

(d)   Four 15-year-old girls have been caught with drugs. The drugs are cannabis and LSD. Three of the girls have only small amounts of the drugs, although one has been cautioned already when cannabis was found previously. The others have no history of offending. One of the girls is found to have a large quantity of drugs in her bedroom. The police suspect she has been dealing, but there is no other evidence for this. All the girls come from well-off families, but they are regarded by their families and schools as 'quite rebellious' and difficult. All are doing well at school, however, and the one with the large quantity of drugs is expected to do very well.

(e)   A boy of 16 has a record of twenty other offences. These are for various crimes, including stealing, taking and driving away of cars, and assault. He is unemployed and lives with his mother and step-father. His real father is in prison. The current offence involved breaking into a house and stealing a video.

7.5 Rights to education

All children have a right to education from the age of 5 to the age of 16. Beyond 16 there is further and higher education for those who choose to stay on and who have the qualifications needed for particular courses. Grants are available in some cases to help with the costs of further and higher education (see Chapter 2).

Behaviour problems

In some situations children are **excluded** from school because of their behaviour. The 1986 Education Act set down procedures to cover this. Parents must be informed of the exclusion and told the reasons. Parents have the right to appeal to the local education authority or the governors if they do not agree with the exclusion.

The Department of Education and Science has a parent's charter for children with special needs

Special needs

Children with special needs also have a right to education. The 1981 Education Act defines special educational needs as 'learning difficulties, greater than those experienced by the majority of children, or which hinder the child from benefiting in education'.

As far as possible, the local education authority must educate children with learning difficulties in ordinary schools. In deciding whether or not to do this, the law says the local authority should take account of the needs of the child, the views of the parents, the needs of the other children and the efficient use of resources.

In a minority of cases the authority will carry out a formal assessment. This is a process known as **statementing**. The authority must tell the parents that the assessment is going to be done, and must allow the parents to add their views to those of the teachers, the educational psychologist and others. The parents will be given the name of someone in the authority who will be able to help them by supplying information.

WORDCHECK

statementing Formal assessment by the local education authority of a child thought to have learning difficulties.

Finding out more: educational rights

★ For detailed information on exclusion and all other aspects of educational rights, contact: The Advisory Centre for Education (ACE).

TO FIND OUT

1 Find out about local policy on children with learning difficulties. First contact the local education authority to discover its policy.

2 Contact a few primary and secondary schools to find out whether they would accept a child with a learning difficulty. Use specific examples, for instance a child who is blind, a child with cerebral palsy and in a wheelchair, and a child with Down's syndrome. Compare the responses of the primary and secondary schools.

3 Contact the local college of further education to see what facilities are available there.

TO THINK ABOUT

What is the best way to educate children with learning difficulties?

- What are the advantages and the disadvantages of educating children with learning difficulties within mainstream schools?

- Do you have any personal experience of learning difficulties, such as may result from Down's syndrome, blindness or inability to walk? What recommendations would *you* make?

CASE STUDIES

Imagine you have clients in the following situations. What advice, help and support would you give?

(a) Pam is worried about her daughter, aged 8. Marie seems slow to learn and is already behind the other children at school in reading and writing.

(b) James is 13 and very disruptive at school. He has been suspended several times and the headteacher is suggesting that he should not remain at the school.

(c) Robert is 11 and has cerebral palsy. So far he has been educated in an ordinary primary school. Now there is a choice between a large comprehensive school, with little in the way of special facilities, and a special school for children with physical disabilities. This has a good reputation but would entail a long journey.

Appendix: useful addresses and helplines

Addresses

ACCEPT Clinic 200 Seagrave Road, London SW6 1RQ.
Action on Alcohol Abuse *See* **Triple A.**
ADFAM National 82 Brompton Road, London SW7 3LQ.
Advisory Centre for Education, The (ACE) 18 Victoria Park Square, London E2 9PB.
Age Concern England Astral House, 1268 London Road, London SW16 4EJ.
Air Transport Users Committee 129 Kingsway, London WC2B 2NN.
Al-Anon Family Groups 61 Great Dover Street, London SE1 4YF.
ALATEEN 61 Great Dover Street, London SE1 4YF.
Alcohol Concern 305 Gray's Inn Road, London WC1X 8QF.
Alcoholics Anonymous (AA) PO B1, Stonebow House, Stonebow, York YO1 2NJ.
Anglia Secure Homes Halifax Chambers, 145a Connaught Avenue, Frinton, Essex CO13 9AH.
Association of Community Health Councils 30 Drayton Park, London N5 1PB.
Association of Therapeutic Communities 146 Charterhouse Square, London EC1M 6AX.

Barnardo's Tanners Lane, Barkingside, Ilford, Essex IG6 1QG.
Black HIV and AIDS Network BM MCC, London WC1N 3XX.
Blackliners PO Box 74, London SW12 9JY.
British Acupuncture Association 22 Hockley Road, Rayleigh, Essex SS6 8EB.
British Airports Authority Gatwick Airport, Gatwick, West Sussex RH6 0HZ.
British Association for Counselling (BAC) 1 Regent Place, Rugby, Warwickshire CV21 2PJ.
British Association for Psychotherapists 121 Hendon Lane, London N3 3PR.
British Association of Cancer United Patients 3 Bath Place, Rivington Street, London EC2A 3JR.
British Chiropractors' Association 5 First Avenue, Chelmsford, Essex CM1 1RX.
British Medical Acupuncture Society 67–69 Chancery Lane, London WC2A 1AF.
British Medical Association BMA House, Tavistock Square, London WC1H 9JP.
British Homeopathic Association 27a Devonshire Street, London W1N 1RJ.

Cancer Relief Anchor House, 15–19 Britten Street, London SW3 3TZ.
Carers National Association 29 Chilworth Mews, London W2 3RG.
Central Council for Jewish Social Service 221 Golders Green Road, London NW11 6DW.
Child Poverty Action Group 1–5 Bath Street, London EC1V 9PY.
Civil Aviation Authority (Printing and Publications Service) PO Box 41, Cheltenham, Gloucestershire GL50 2BN.
Commission for Racial Equality (CRE) Elliot House, 10–12 Allington Street, London SW1E 5EH.
Community Care Carew House, Station Road, Wallington, Surrey SM6 0DX.
Community Self-Build Agency, The 18 Northampton Square, London EC1V 0AJ.

Community Transport Association Highbank, Halton Street, Hyde, Cheshire SK14 2NY.

Counsel and Care for the Elderly 131 Middlesex Street, London E1 7JF.

DAWN (Drugs, Alcohol, Women, Nationally) Omnibus Workspace, 39 North Road, London N7 9DP.

Depressives Anonymous 36 Chestnut Avenue, Beverley, North Humberside HU17 9QU.

DIAL-UK 117 High Street, Clay Cross, Derbyshire S45 9DZ (*tel.* 0246 250055).

Disability Alliance 1st Floor East, Universal House, 88–94 Wentworth Street, London E1 7SA.

Disabled Living Foundation 380–384 Harrow Road, London W9 2HU.

Drinkwatchers c/o ACCEPT Clinic, 200 Seagrave Road, London SW6 1RQ.

DSS Information Division (Leaflets Unit) Block 4, Government Buildings, Honeypot Lane, Stanmore, Middlesex HA7 1AY.

Employment Service Rockingham House, 123 West Street, Sheffield S1 4ER.

Families Anonymous 310 Finchley Road, London NW3 7AG.

Family Fund PO Box 50, York YO1 1UY.

Family Policy Studies Centre 231 Baker Street, London NW1 6XE.

Federation of Claimants Unions 296 Bethnal Green Road, London E2 0AG.

General Council and Register of Osteopaths 1–4 Suffolk Street, London SW1Y 4HG.

General Dental Council 37 Wimpole Street, London W1M 8DQ.

Global Homes Southern Ltd Global House, 38–40 High Street, West Wickham, Kent BR4 0WJ.

Health Information Line PO Box 1577, London NW1 3DW.

Health Publications Unit No. 2 Site, Heywood Stores, Manchester Road, Heywood, Lancashire OL10 2PZ.

Holiday Care Service 2 Old Bank Chambers, Station Road, Horley, Surrey RH6 9HW.

Hospice Information Service 51–59 Lawrie Park Road, Sydenham, London SE26 9DZ.

Housing Corporation, The 149 Tottenham Court Road, London W1P 0BN.

Independent Living Fund Box 183, Nottingham NG8 3RD.

Institute for Complementary Medicine 21 Portland Place, London W1N 3AF.

London Dial-a-Ride Users Association St Margaret's, 25 Leighton Road, London NW5 2QD.

London Housing Aid Centre, The *See* **SHAC**.

London Regional Transport Unit for Disabled Passengers 55 Broadway, London SW1H 0BD.

Medical Advisory Service, The 10 Barley Mow Passage, London W4 4PH.

MENCAP Holiday Office 119 Drake Street, Rochdale, Lancashire OL16 1PZ.

MIND 22 Harley Street, London W1N 2ED.

Motability Gate House, Westgate, Harlow, Essex CM20 1HR.

NAM Publications Ltd PO Box 99, London SW2 1EL.

Narcotics Anonymous PO Box 704, London SW10 0RN.

National Advisory Unit, The 35 Fountain Street, Manchester M2 2AF.

National Association of Health Authorities and Trusts Birmingham Research Park, Vincent Drive, Birmingham B15 2SQ.

National Childminding Association (NCMA) 8 Mason's Hill, Bromley, Kent BR2 9EY.

National Children's Bureau 8 Wakeley Street, London EC1V 7QE.

National Federation for Housing Associations 175 Grays Inn Road, London WC1X 8UP.
National Schizophrenia Fellowship 78 Surbiton Road, Surrey KT6 4NS.
Nationwide Housing Trust Ltd New Oxford House, High Holborn, London WC1V 6PW.

Open College, The Freepost, PO Box 35, Abingdon OX14 3BR.

Positively Women 333 Gray's Inn Road, London WC1X 8PX.
Pre-school Playgroups Association (PPA) 61–63 King's Cross Road, London WC1X 9LL.

RADAR *See* Royal Association for Disability and Rehabilitation.
Retirement Care Ltd Tubs Hill House, Sevenoaks, Kent TN13 1DB.
Richmond Fellowship 8 Addison Road, London W14 6DL.
Royal Association for Disability and Rehabilitation (RADAR) 25 Mortimer Street, London W1N 8AB.

SCODA (Standing Conference on Drug Abuse) 1 Hatton Place, London EC1N 8ND.
Scottish Aids Monitor National Office, PO Box 48, Edinburgh EH1 5SA.
SHAC (The London Housing Centre) 189a Old Brompton Road, London SW5 0AR.
Shelter 88 Old Street, London EC1V 9HU.
Society of Chiropodists, The 53 Welbeck Street, London W1M 7HE.
Society of Homœopaths 47a Canada Grove, Bognor Regis, West Sussex PO21 1OW.

Terence Higgins Trust 52–54 Gray's Inn Road, London WC1X 6LT.
TRANX 25a Masons Avenue, Wealdstone, Harrow, Middlesex HA3 5AH.
Triple A (Action on Alcohol Abuse) Livingstone House, 11 Carteret Street, London SW11 9DL.

Unemployment Unit 409 Brixton Road, London SW9 7OQ.

Well-care Room 1214, Queens Building, Heathrow Airport, Hounslow, Middlesex TW6 1JH.
Women's Therapy Centre 6 Manor Gardens, London W7.

Helplines

BUPA Medicall 0839 100 100.

Department of Social Security General advice on benefits:

- English: 0800 666 555;
- Urdu: 0800 289 555;
- Punjabi: 0800 521 360;
- Welsh: 0800 289 011;
- Northern Ireland: 0800 616 757;
- Disability benefits: 0800 181 794.

Healthcall 0800 600 600.

Motor Neurone Disease Phoneline 0800 626262.

National AIDS Helpline 0800 567 123.

Index